Christ and Revolution

CHRIST AND REVOLUTION

MARCEL CLEMENT

Translated from the French by
Alice von Hildebrand with Marilyn Teichert

ARLINGTON HOUSE·PUBLISHERS
NEW ROCHELLE, N. Y.

Library of Congress Cataloging in Publication Data

Clément, Marcel.
    Christ and revolution.

    Translation of Le Christ et la révolution.
    Includes bibliographical references.
    1. Sociology, Christian. 2. Socialism. I. Title.
BT738.C5513   261.7   74-3060
ISBN 0-87000-233-3

Contents

Introduction

CHRIST AND REVOLUTION

A Strategic Turn

In the course of the last weeks of the year 1971, three documents were made public in Rome, Madrid and Paris. Taken singly, each one of them could be interpreted, strange as it might be, as a transitory inflection of the relationship existing between the Church and the world, or more exactly, of the relationship existing between the Church and politics. But their simultaneous appearance and the outspoken campaign for a political "liberation" in the name of the Gospel, which followed during the first months of 1972, have nevertheless suggested to religious observers that we were not dealing with isolated happenings, but rather with a strategic change of direction initiated by the action of various ecclesiastical milieux, and by militant Catholics and Protestants.

Three Documents

I am referring to the publication in close succession of the synodal document about justice in the world (*La Croix*, December 14); of the study made by the Protestant Federation of France and entitled "Church and Power" (*Le Monde*, December 19); and finally of the text drafted by the Commission of Justice and Peace in the Spanish Church, on the occasion of "The World Day of Peace" (*Le Monde*, December 23).

It should be clear that my bringing together these three documents should not lead to identifying them. One of them had been endorsed, paragraph by paragraph, by vote of the bishops of the synod. The reformed document presents itself, not as an encyclical, but rather as a plan of action. Furthermore, it provoked strong reactions on the part of high Protestant personalities. The third seems to involve only the Episcopal Commission of Spain. Moreover, the matters discussed, even though related, are distinct.

But the three documents share common features which deserve close attention: the tone, the thesis, and the point.

The Tone

To begin with, the tone is unusual; it is pessimistic. A few quotations of this synodal document will reflect faithfully the general climate of this study. It asserts the right and the duty "of denouncing unjust situations when man's basic rights and even his salvation require it." It states that, "Our denunciation can carry assent only to the extent that it is borne out in our lives." It denounces " . . . a body of injustices which constitute the core of the problems of today." It proclaims the necessity "of awakening a critical faculty which will bring men to reflect on the society in which they live," etc.

The Protestant document is no more positive in tone: "Both the system and the ideology under which we live are inacceptable in their current state." They must be denounced, and opposed to them should be "a radical rejection of the status quo."

The document drafted by the Spanish commission, in its turn, expresses its "concern about the unsatisfactory realization of the rights of the human person." It praises the prophets who "have denounced those who, peacefully settled in their comfort, hate everyone who allows himself to criticize, or to express himself in severe terms." The commission affirms further that the Church "must take the risk of denouncing the present injustice, even if, in so doing, it were to incite the criticism, incomprehension, contempt and persecution of the powerful ones of this earth, against its hierarchy or laity."

This is a far cry from the positive and hopeful note of the documents of Vatican II. It is a far cry, too, from the desire neither to condemn nor to denounce, but rather to treat one's adversaries with goodness, according to the formula of *Gaudium et spes.* "Respect and love must also be extended to those who think or act differently in matters social, political or religious. Moreover, the more we strive to understand their points of view from within, with benevolence and love, the easier will our dialogue with them become." At any rate, the tone of the three documents mentioned above does not reflect the tone of Vatican II. Confidence and fraternal correction have been replaced by the bitterness of denunciation. (This word keeps reappearing like a *leit-motiv*.)

The Thesis

Let us examine their thesis. Without being rigorously identical in the three documents, it is obviously similar.

The synodal document multiplies general descriptions of injustice in this world: "We have been able to gauge the grievous injustices which throw a network of dominations, oppressions, exploitations, around the earth." The culpability for these is not directly attributed to men, but rather to "structures." The oppressed "are crushed by systems and unjust mechanisms." Or again, "Social structures create objective obstacles to the conversion of hearts."

Why are these structures so contrary to the justice of the Gospel? We must admit that the synodal document is not very explicit about them. But it takes up the theme and the vocabulary of dialectic analysis. "The dividing forces and the antagonisms intensify their pressure from day to day." "The control of three-fourths of all revenues, investments and business" belongs "to only one third of the world population." Without pronouncing the words "private ownership of production means," it nevertheless insinuates: "The early Church lived . . . conversion to faith, to Christ and to fraternal love realized in a reciprocal aid, to the community of goods." It insinuates further, "A part of the human family live submerged in a mentality that beatifies possession." It seems to endorse the idea that, "In the so-called socialistic world, the will to promotion expresses itself primarily in the struggle for the forms of demands and expression engendered by the evolution of the economic system."

But all this is only briefly sketched, and more subtle than outspoken. One receives the impression that either the bishops have failed to agree on the unequivocal affirmation that the Gospel implies socialism, or that they are somewhat embarrassed by the teaching of all the popes on the natural right of ownership. Incidentally, one brief paragraph tends to "balance" all this, concerning "those who suffer persecution for their faith," immediately followed by a sharp passage: "Cases of torture are well known, particularly with respect to political prisoners."

The thesis of the Protestant document manifests a commitment. In the given context it is unmistakable that the capitalist system is referred to: "By 'reigning economic and political powers' we mean the system and the ideology—either implicit or explicit—which structure the society in which we live." The language of Marxist dialectic is employed without subterfuge: " . . . system and ideology which are inacceptable in their present state, and which, because of their very contradiction call . . . either for a daring spirit of reform or for a revolutionary overthrow."

The word is out. We are truly dealing with a radical rejection of the capitalistic system, formulated according to the Marxist terminology. The alternative offered to the Christian Protestant is either "a daring spirit of reform," or bluntly "revolutionary" action. In practice, if these words have any meaning, they signify, "Vote for socialists or communists in the next elections," or "put up barricades."

The text of the Spanish episcopal commission goes just as far in theory, for it denounces the situation "provoked and maintained by the materialistic system of the capitalistic brand which dominates our society." It asks the faithful to examine their consciences "to see how far our participation in injustices extends— or, what amounts to the same thing—our complacency, and to what extent we share the wrong ideals of peace."

Such is the thesis. In spite of a diversity of means and perspectives, it undoubtedly reflects a common orientation; a total refusal of a system based on private ownership of the means of production, which is identified with materialism.

10

The Point

Let us now examine the point that is the clearest in these three texts. The point is identical: it insinuates or denotes a condemnation in the name of the Gospel of the system of private property and production.

The synodal text goes quite far: "The mission to preach the Gospel demands, today, a radical commitment to the total liberation of man, now, in the very reality of his existence in the world. If the Christian message of love and justice fails to realize itself in action for justice in this world, it will hardly seem credible to the man of today." So, the apostolate of faith would demand in practice the efficaciousness of the social message, and the message of the Gospel would imply a liberation, the context of which indicates that it is not only spiritual but also temporal. "The struggle for justice and the participation in the transformation of the world seem to us to be an essential dimension of the preaching of the Gospel, which is the Church's mission for the redemption of humanity, and its liberation from any oppressive situation."

The Protestant text is no less explicit. "Let there be no misunderstanding about this: it is clear that an insertion into the social body, whatever this may be, is implied in the Gospel of Incarnation. The whole problem is that this insertion be meaningful, i.e., critical and questioning of whatever in the system is incompatible with the hope the Gospel brings us."

The Spanish text is signed and promulgated by a commission, "Justice and Peace," depending on the Spanish Church and published on the occasion of "The World Day of Peace." It stresses from beginning to end that the Gospel contains a temporal message which requires social justice in so far as it is a system, and that the "materialistic system" of the capitalist type is incompatible with the Church's message. Spain has been exposed to such sufferings that, in a discourse delivered in Leon on December 18, Mr. Alfredo Lopez, Secretary of State in the Department of Justice, could not refrain from ascertaining that there is "a new religious mentality," which tends to see "the Kingdom of God in the realization of social progress" and "to view Christ as a precursor of modern, socialist struggles."

11

Seven Questions

In a period in which the words "Christ" and "Revolution" are daily paired together, the tone, the thesis and the point of the three documents mentioned above raises quite a few questions. It is important, it is urgent, it is legitimate to formulate those which express, on a largely ecumenical plane, the profound questioning of the consciences of a good many Christians.

1. In what sense and to what extent can one speak of a social message implied in the Gospel?

2. What are the various meanings of the word "liberation" in the contemporary intellectual and social context? Which of these coincide with and which are opposed to the social message implied in the Gospel?

3. Is the identification of Christ's Gospel with the call to revolution[1] compatible with what we know Christian faith to be?

4. From the point of view of the preaching of the Gospel, can we consider the right of ownership as an objective obstacle to the proclamation of salvation?

5. Is socialism with a "human face" realizable and compatible with the natural order inscribed in human nature?

6. Is socialism with a "human face" compatible with a simple "sense of faith"?

7. Can the present menace of totalitarianism help us discover the essential features of a modern society worthy of God and man?

At a time in which many assume that the message of Christ can be identified with the call to revolution, it is clear that these seven questions express one crucial aspect of the "interior dialogue within the ecclesial community," and at the same time "with those outside" ("our separated brethren") wished by Paul VI in his encyclical *Ecclesiam suam*. This dialogue is all the more important in that all those who understand the major importance

---

1. I wish to express my profound gratitude to the Rev. Fr. Panici, S.J. who, having preached during the Lenten Season at Notre Dame in Paris, in 1945, published under the title "Christ and Revolution," and has authorized me to use this title for the present work.

of political involvement today know that various elections loom on the horizon whose outcome could either ring the knell of our lost liberty or the *Te Deum* of our liberty preserved from destruction.

The seven chapters which follow will examine these questions one by one. They shall hopefully contribute, if not to the forestallment of the struggle, at least to clarification of the issues involved. In short, I wish to highlight the points at issue, so that if a choice is to be made, it will not be dictated by the hammering of propaganda, but rather by a reflection steeped in spiritual freedom.

Christ and Revolution

1

THE SOCIAL MESSAGE
OF THE GOSPEL

Two Interventions in the Synod
Which Method are We to Use?
Spiritual Liberation
Evangelical Poverty
Social Message

In what sense and to what extent can one speak of a social message implied in the Gospel?

From the very outset, the synodal document consecrated to "justice in this world" poses a problem of conscience to every Christian, because of the following statement:

> The struggle for justice and the participation in the transformation of the world appear to us fully as an essential dimension of the preaching of the Gospel which is the mission of the Church for the salvation of humanity and its liberation from any oppressive situation.

This problem is raised by Father Sorge in an article of December 1971, published in *Civilitá Cattolica*. This problem is, he tells us, the determination of the relationship existing between human freedom and the salvation brought by Jesus Christ. Taking into account the ambiguity contained in the notion of "human liberation," one can simply formulate the difficulty in the following terms: In what sense, and to what extent, can one speak of a social message implied in the Gospel?

Two Interventions in the Synod

In this respect, Father Sorge quotes two interventions made at the synod which contain, at least potentially, two divergent answers, not to say radically opposed.

One of these interventions came from Cardinal Henrique y Tarancon, now Archbishop of Madrid. He affirmed in particular that "the salvation described in the Scriptures is not a salvation outside of history, to which one should afterwards add justice as something that either precedes or follows . . . . Among the present forms of sin, one should list some social facts, such as colonialism, cultural or economic domination, oppression, etc. The grace of God through which man is liberated from sin is not only given to him individually, but also socially, through the ecclesial community, so that it may impregnate the whole social reality. One does not solve the problems posed by the liberative action of the Church in the social domain either in abstracting from the reality of the world, or in introducing a separation of salvation from justice."

According to Cardinal Henrique y Tarancon, the salvation "described" by the Scriptures, if applied today, aims at "social facts like colonialism, economic or cultural liberation, oppression, etc." And this conception of an historical salvation realizing itself through the reform of structures rests on a theology of grace. The latter is not essentially given to society through the conversion of hearts. Directly spread somehow through "the ecclesial community," it is the latter which will transform the reality of the world in impregnating it.

The opposite intervention mentioned by Father Sorge is the one of Cardinal Hoeffner, Archbishop of Cologne. The cardinal, who spoke in the name of the German episcopate, declared, "In the New Testament, 'justice' signifies the just life of man before God, or the justification of man through Christ. Evangelical freedom consists not in the liberation of man from the slavery of other men, but in the liberation of man from his own sins, through

18

Jesus Christ. I doubt whether it can be said that the liberation and development of peoples are integral parts of redemption."

In short, Cardinal Hoeffner defines the justice Christ brought us as an interior justice, the liberty through which he frees us as an interior liberty, the kingdom he revealed to us as an interior kingdom. It goes without saying that the growth of this justice, of this liberty, of this kingdom in the souls is accompanied by great benefits in man's exterior life. But the type of justice preached and brought by Christ does not essentially coincide with temporal justice in history. The latter type of justice often called today "liberation" or "development" has strictly speaking *nothing to do with the Gospel.*

It is hardly necessary to underline how great is our concern and our suffering in witnessing that cardinals clash on such a fundamental question as the one of the overall significance of the Gospel. This apprehension is intensified by a remark of Father Sorge in the article previously quoted: the question raised has not yet been essentially cleared up. But in fact, concrete initiatives and practical orientations multiply themselves, as if Cardinal Henrique y Taracon's thesis, which is certainly a new one, had already been admitted.

In this difficult situation, both intellectually and spiritually, the four gospels should be our beacon.

What Method Are We to Employ?

In order to examine the question, "Do the gospels contain a social message? If yes, what is it?" the first difficulty we encounter is that of our method of approach.

One way of proceeding, which is frequently used, consists of tracing in any of the four evangelists quotations which either directly or analogically point to social, economic, or political questions. Such is the procedure adopted by Harvey Cox in *The Secular City*. He writes:

" . . . the Church's ministry is simply the continuation of Jesus' ministry. It cooperates and participates in the ministry of Jesus. But what is the character of Jesus' ministry? Jesus himself described it in these terms:

19

The spirit of the Lord is upon me,
Because he has anointed me to preach good news to the poor
He has sent me to proclaim release to the captives and
recovering to the blind,
To set at liberty those who are oppressed,
To proclaim the acceptable year of the Lord.

Having summarized in this one quotation what Harvey Cox calls "the character of Jesus' ministry," he interprets it literally in its meaning for social liberation, and defines as follows the "kerygmatic" function of the Church:

> It has no plan for rebuilding the world. It has only the signal to flash that the One who frees slaves and summons men to maturity is still in business.[1]

No effort is required to understand that such an exegetic method is inacceptable. It begins by attributing directly to Jesus what is in fact, according to the context, a quotation which he makes of the prophet Isaiah (61:1-2). It isolates this quotation from the progressive development of Jesus' own message in the course of the three years of his public life. This development sheds the new light of the Gospel on the prophecy of Isaiah. Harvey Cox propagates the impression that Jesus truly aimed at a social revolution. This is so much the case that finally the sentence, "He who liberates slaves is still in business," is interpreted to mean that during his earthly existence, Jesus worked toward the temporal abolition of slavery. But Jesus, who accepted the type of death reserved to slaves, neither spoke nor acted during his earthly life for the temporal abolition of the institution of slavery.[2]

The very same method is used more seriously and in a more subtle fashion by Pierre Bigo, in his book entitled *The Social Doc-*

---

[1] Harvey Cox, *The Secular City*, The Macmillan Company, New York, 1965, pp. 126-127. (Quotation from Luke 4:18, 19.)

[2] This should not make us overlook the fact that a whole civilization is born out of the infusion of spiritual life into humanity; this has made possible an unceasing improvement of justice.

trine of the Church.[3] In a chapter entitled "The Gospel," he singles out mainly:

> the theme of the "small" and of the poor
> the warning to the rich who refuse to give fair wages
> the evangelical theme of friendship which shares
> the condemnation of wealth
> the chapter on money
> charity.

Pierre Bigo's work is not devoid of attraction. But here again, the method is faulty. It selects quotations, classifies, and interprets them. But it does not throw satisfactory light upon them because it fails to place them accurately in the historical development of Jesus' message.

This critical reflection is not useless. It spurs us toward the only method which seems capable of answering the question previously posed. This method consists of giving precedence to an examination of the progressive aspect of the revelation Jesus brought to humanity, over any exegesis and any commentary on evangelical quotations related to social questions. This examination will shed light on all the rest.

The narration of the life and words of Jesus, when re-read in the four evangelists in succession, enables us to gain a general perspective. The actions and discourses of the Lord are to be placed beyond and above a simple juxtaposition of aphorisms, precepts, counsels and miracles. There is a gradation, a succession of stages, both intellectual and spiritual. To be more exact, there is a pedagogical method used by Jesus with the crowds, and a different one for the apostles. The progressive order of what he did and what he said is not unimportant. More than the factuality of gestures and words, it is this very order which is prophetic. In the last analysis, it is this order which manifests what must be called, even though it has too human a ring, the plan of Jesus. It is this method which I shall try to apply in order to answer the question raised above, for it will unveil the dynamism of the pedagogical

---

[3] Pierre Bigo, *The Social Doctrine of the Church*, pp. 15-26.

method used by Jesus before examining the social, economic, or political aspects of his teaching.

Spiritual Liberation

Luke as well as Matthew, speaks of the infancy of Christ. But all four evangelists agree in beginning the narrative of the public life of Jesus with the preaching of John the Baptist. No misunderstanding is possible about this. This introduction resounds like a call to interiority, to recollection, to repentance.

Perhaps it is in Mark's gospel that this affirmation is most striking. After having entitled his text, "Beginning of the Good News of Jesus Christ, Son of God," he continues, almost without transition, "John baptized in the wilderness, and preached the baptism of repentance for the remission of sins."

The tone is set. There is one in the desert, the visible sign of a silence in which the soul can hearken to God speaking intimately to the very core of our spirit. The preaching of John the Baptist is of a moral order; he exhorts those who surround him to listen to the voice speaking in the very core of their souls, to become conscious of their sinfulness. His baptism is one of repentance.

It is within the context of this spiritual struggle to which John the Baptist invites us that we are to understand the exterior harshness with which he addresses both the Pharisees and the Saducees: "You generation of vipers . . .!" he exclaims; and he makes them understand that only a complete change of their innermost attitude can rescue them from eternal damnation.

Who were the Pharisees? They were members of the purest sect, the strictest and most literal observers of the law, taught by the Scribes, doctors of the law. The Saducees, on the other hand, were very lax in their observance of the law; they were characterized by their religious tepidity, and were much more preoccupied with the advantages to be gained from an openness toward the enticing Greek world than with the implicit dangers of such an overture.

Thus the opposing forces of the spiritual combat are clearly presented: on the one hand penance, but in spirit and truth—not tainted by the legalistic pride of the Pharisees; and on the other hand, openness to the world, but not the lax and indiscriminate openness of the Saducees.

The Son, as he appears on the scene, is announced by the prophet. But he is invested by the Father, and in a miraculous way. This fact must be insisted upon. He is God's Chosen One, His Messenger, even if it is John the Baptist who has made him known and baptized him. All four evangelists tell of the Spirit descending in the form of a dove and the Voice from heaven proclaiming that Jesus is the Son, the Beloved of the Father.

This beginning speaks eloquently. What it announces is neither a political nor a social action. It prepares a spiritual work, and more deeply yet, a mystical one, i.e., at the center of the mystery of the soul.

Immediately we see Jesus begin his public life, not by intellectual, sociological or economic studies, but by spiritual exercises. In short, he inaugurates his action on souls by what, today, we would call a retreat—even a closed retreat. He withdraws into the seclusion of the desert; the synoptic gospels tell us that he is led by the Spirit into the desert "in order to be tempted." There he spends forty days fasting and praying.

Let us speak plainly: The devil exists, and the angels exist—the rebel angels and the faithful ones. If they did not exist, Jesus' struggle would not have been spiritual, but rather social. His fasting would have been undertaken in order to impress the public, and would resemble the fastings we see perpetrated today, even in churches . . . and announced in newspapers! The Lord Himself has warned us against ideological hunger strikes! He has commanded us not to publicize our fasts but to fast " . . . in such fashion that you will be seen not by men, but by your Father . . . ." (Mat. 6:18). What is in question here is a truly spiritual struggle, a mystical action.

It is through prayer and fasting that demons can be cast out. The account of the temptations is as precise in Matthew as it is in Luke. It conveys the spirit of Christ's life. It was to be a combat, not social, but spiritual. Jesus, the True God, reveals to us the invisible world: the devil exists. Satan acts on our appetites, our lusts, our pride, in order to seduce us. Jesus, a true man, shows us how man can, through prayer and fasting, sustain spiritual combat—the interior fight against principalities and powers.

Harvey Cox states unequivocally: "These 'principalities and powers' actually signify all the forces in a culture which cripple and corrupt human freedom." What are these forces? During the age of superstition, man imagined them to be invisible. "In the tribal era which colors much of the New Testament, they were perceived as demons, spirits, and astral forces." Now that man is liberated from superstitions, he knows that what blinds him are sociological and archaic structures with badly adjusted mechanics. In particular, " . . . Ids and economic pressures still roam through history."[4]

One begins to perceive the enormity of what is at stake when angels are no longer mentioned in sermons and catechisms or approached in a purely literary manner, shamefully or hesitantly. At the same time the accent is put on "the fight for justice" which the Christian is called upon to enter. The Christian is thereby inevitably led to consider penance and prayer as inefficacious consolations in the social domain and even, under the influence of socialist propaganda, as diversions from the "real" action that should be urgently undertaken with a view to bringing about the complete liberation of man. Step by step the Christian religion becomes, in fact, a setting for atheistic propaganda.

Is it not at the very heart of religion that one witnesses today the replacement of the teaching on the invisible world by the study of social questions, of economic pressures, and by a more or less explicit invitation to commit oneself to revolutionary action? This is, at any rate, the case in numerous churches.

All this may be very fashionable indeed. It can all be explained by a confusion of spirits which will be more or less lasting. *But one must not hesitate to state categorically that this is not the Catholic faith.* Indeed, the Credo speaks of the visible "and invisible" world. The Lateran Council teaches that the only true God has "created each creature from nothing, spiritual and corporal, namely, angelic and mundane."[5] This has been the

---

4 *Loc. cit.,* pp. 126, 127.

5 Denziger, *The Sources of Catholic Dogma,* tr. by Roy Deferrari (St. Louis: B. Herder Books Co., 1957), No. 428, p. 169.

consistent teaching of the Councils of Lyon,[6] of Florence,[7] of Vatican I,[8] and of Vatican II.[9] It is the actual teaching of Paul VI who, in his profession of faith, pays homage to God, the creator of visible "and of invisible things like the pure spirits called angels."

The powers of Heaven and Hell exist. Man is the object of the combat taking place between them. This is also true on a social plane. The Eternal Word became flesh in order to carry on this fight within human nature. It is in order that we may partake of His victory by Him, through Him, with Him and in Him, that the Son paid the price of redemption on the cross.

He came, therefore, not primarily or simply to bring about political, social or economic liberation, necessary as this may be, seen in a Christian light.

"We hold with the Council of Trent," Paul VI teaches, "that original sin is transmitted with human nature, not by imitation, but by propagation, and that it is thus proper to everyone."[10] Except for Mary, each man is stained by original sin. He has fallen into the bondage of the devil—the invisible enemy of humanity who hates the human race and endeavors to undermine man's freedom in order that he might encourage in man a passion for destruction, and for self-destruction.

Seen in this light, Jesus did come to liberate man, not from slavery to other men (this type of subjection is well known to man, who, when he suffers under it rebels against it), but from subjugation to Satan and his angels. This liberation, which is essentially spiritual, constitutes the supreme and matchless scheme of His love. Jesus has come, therefore, to redeem men, through the sacrifice of the cross, from "original sin and all the personal sins committed by each one of us."[11]

Christ's passion and crucifixion were required to ac-

---

[6] Ibid., No. 461, p. 183.
[7] Ibid., No. 994, p. 302.
[8] Ibid., Numbers 1783, 1802, 599.
[9] *Lumen Gentium,* No. 50.
[10] Pope Paul VI, *Credo.*
[11] *Ibid.*

complish this. But that was not sufficient. Man, being free, had to learn through Jesus to cooperate with his own salvation. Each man had to know the good news of salvation. Each man had to receive the good news of salvation in order to apply it to himself, i.e., to fight the infernal powers with the help of Christ.

Thus, it is *not* within a cultural context of tribal origin, or of superstitions understandable in the Middle Ages that we see the devil overcome by Jesus in the desert as in the three synoptic gospels; or that we hear of the liberation of a man possessed of demons in both Mark and Luke ("Be silent and leave this man")—the liberation of the possessed of Gadara again in the three synoptic gospels.

One cannot, by mere folkloric tradition, explain the insistence with which the devils themselves denounced Jesus as being the Son of God; this cannot shed light on Jesus' explanation to the apostles of how an impure spirit, driven out of a man's soul, goes out to seek seven other spirits, more wicked than himself, in order to reestablish his dominion. It is not a mere mythological or symbolic formulation by which Luke and John specify the moment in which "Satan entered into Judas."

These statements and many similar ones are made in order that Jesus' disciples might know, not merely that there are good spirits and evil ones—they never doubted this fact—but that Jesus has power over them. They had to be given courage for a spiritual battle. And Luke notes with precision the disciples' amazement upon their returning from a mission: "The seventy-two came back rejoicing. 'Lord,' they said, 'even the devils submit to us when we use your name.' He said to them, 'I watched Satan fall like lightning from heaven. Yes, I have given you power to tread underfoot serpents and scorpions and the whole strength of the enemy; nothing shall ever hurt you. Yet do not rejoice that the spirits submit to you; rejoice rather that your names are written in heaven.' "[12]

The core of this message of spiritual liberation resides not in the power to exorcize, conferred by Jesus in particular cases

---

[12] Luke 10:17-20.

throughout the history of the Church. Rather exorcisms give more exterior testimony to the fact that He who possesses and can exercise such a power over demons can also grant his disciples the strength to resist temptations or to stand up again when they have fallen.

The precondition for spiritual liberation is spiritual combat. To wage this battle we must perceive a new meaning to words, an inner, spiritual meaning.

Progression and Poverty

The Jews indeed expected a messenger from God. But the legalistic exegesis of the prophetic writings presented him under the aspect of a faultless authority who would bring about the reign of justice in the Name of the Lord, Jahweh, and instigate a complete change, a general renewal. Some dreamed of a warrior-king who, like Judas Maccabeus, would liberate the Jewish people from the Roman occupation. The more spiritually minded imagined that other nations (the Gentiles) would be converted to Judaism. The nationalistic dreamed of a temporal conquest of other peoples. All agreed in the hope that they would be subjected to Israel "like a stool under the foot of a powerful man."[13]

Against this background, the task of Jesus was not an easy one. Even the apostles are not free of political ambition. They expect Jesus to reestablish the kingdom; they quarrel over questions of priorities.

Revelation will have to be progressive. From one point of view it manifests itself in a movement from the lower to the higher. Jesus takes a material example as his point of departure in order to clarify its spiritual significance.

This is the method he uses concerning his own identity. He does not bluntly proclaim at the outset his identity as the Son of God. Had he done this he would have incurred the immediate opposition of some and encouraged the ambition of others. Consequently, he starts out by following the lines of the prophecy of

---

[13] Cf. Père Lagrange, *Messianism Among the Jews* (Paris, 1909).

27

Daniel and speaks of "the Son of God." When his apostles are sufficiently secure in their faith (although not yet confirmed) he asks them to be discreet, as he does with those he has healed, even with demons, speaking through the possessed. It is only at the very hour in which a temporal deviation of his mission is ruled out that he solemnly and publicly claims, in clear terms, the title of the Son of God when facing his judges.

Similarly, Christ draws those about him away from their concern about their physical health to solicitude for their spiritual health.

Because he heals them, the sick come to him in throngs. It is primarily because of this, at first, that he is spoken of in Galilee. Families come to him with no thought except the cure of those they bring for him to heal.

One day, Jesus paradoxically declares to a paralytic who has been brought to him, "My child, your sins are forgiven." Both Scribes and Pharisees exclaim that this is blasphemy. Jesus retorts, "Why do you have these thoughts in your hearts? Which of these is easier: to say to the paralytic, 'Your sins are forgiven' or to say, 'Get up, pick up your stretcher and walk?' But to prove to you that the Son of Man has authority on earth to forgive sins . . . I order you: get up, pick up your stretcher, and go off home."[14]

Thus, in Cana, Jesus changes water into wine. Twice on the shores of the sea of Tibrias he miraculously multiplies loaves. He thereby not only manifests his love, but also, at the same time, prepares the mind for another miracle, the transsubstantiation at the Last Supper, the bread changed into his body, the wine changed into his blood.

At Jacob's well, he teaches and communicates mystical life to the Samaritan woman in a similar way. He begs her for well water in order to make her understand by analogy that he can create in her soul a well of living water—the source of eternal life.

It is clearly in terms of this way of teaching, leading from the visual meaning to the spiritual one, that one must understand the quotation of Isaiah used too literally by Harvey Cox. The rescue

---

[14] Mark 2:9-10.

spoken of is of the captives of sin, those under the slavery of Satan. It is a spiritual liberation which is in question.

These events, finally, contribute to the understanding that man does not live by bread alone, but by every word that comes from the mouth of God, and that if the food of the Son is to do his Father's will, so must it be for those who, in the Son, recite the prayer to the Father and say to Him, "Thy will be done." They adore and obey in spirit and in truth.

In this progressive revelation of faith, Jesus teaches by means of various analogies and numerous parables that the essential condition for escaping from Satan's power and receiving into the soul the mystery of the Kingdom of God is poverty. Here, as elsewhere, Jesus strives to make his disciples go from the literal to the spiritual sense, or, to put it differently, from the meaning revealed by flesh and blood to the meaning revealed by the Spirit.

In its common usage "poverty" indicates the lack of means to live decently. The poor are the sorrowing, suffering members of the social body and of the Mystical Body. The apprenticeship to poverty, when one's heart is pure, renders one sensitive to the sufferings of others. It grants one, at times, a bewildering generosity. " . . . anyone who wants to become great among you must be your servant, and anyone who wants to be first among you must be slave to all."[15] In short, poverty, accepted and offered up, leads to a human situation which is at the same time the hardest to bear—especially when the head of a family labors under it—and simultaneously, most capable of refining one's heart, to make it sensitive to the sufferings of others, helpful in creating solidarity with others through self-renunciation. This poverty, when accepted, is in a certain sense the natural training ground of the cross of Christ.

This common meaning of poverty occurs in the Gospel. It is not, however, properly speaking, its true evangelical meaning.

It is obvious that the blind, the deaf, the paralyzed, all those whose bodies are not whole are also "poor." It is clear that an orphan, a handicapped child, an abandoned husband, a widow, a

---

[15] Mark 10:43.

29

prisoner, all those frustrated in their affections are also poor, truly poor. It would be meaningless to identify this more general meaning of the word poor with a social class, whatever this may be, or with a material standard of living, whatever it is. Nothing is more odious than to make of evangelical poverty the privilege of a particular social class.

Indeed, evangelical poverty means all forms of privation and frustration humbly accepted, whether they be physical, intellectual, cultural, or social. First and foremost, poverty is destined to play the role of a pedagogical point of reference: in order that, regardless of the particular form poverty may take, Jesus' disciples penetrate into its secret, into the inner disposition, the spiritual attitude of detachment, of "nakedness," and finally of total self-abandonment into the hands of the Father.

Jesus manifests his displeasure toward the rich, i.e., all those who cling to their assets, whether material, carnal, intellectual, affective, social; whether it be power, reputation or self-will. He thereby tries to wake them up. He is not attempting (as some seem to believe today) to enkindle hatred against the bourgeois class! He endeavors to arouse those sated with earthly things—those with limited wealth as well as the very rich—and this in all strata of society.

The rich man is he who refuses to become like a small child. The man who practices perfect poverty is childlike; he claims nothing as his own. He expects everything. Because he knows his father loves him, he believes everything. He hopes all things. He loves all people. Because he is aware of his weakness, his ignorance, his limitations, and his utter dependence on his father, he feeds himself on the bread from his father's hand, on the living word of his father, on his father's will.

The beatitude of the poor in spirit is, in the final anlysis, the perfection of the filial spirit toward the heavenly Father, a loving submission and an act of grace, an unceasing song of thanksgiving. This necessarily implies also the practice of a considerate, indefatigable, fraternal charity.

This explains Jesus' insistent emphasis on the fact that "the Good News is proclaimed to the poor" (Matt. 11:5). And how very poor they are! The deaf, the blind, the lame, the lepers, the paralyzed; the adulterous woman, the Canaanite woman, the Samaritan, the public sinner . . . . No one is excepted from the call to live this filial love for the Father, and this fraternal love for one's brothers in spite of social, racial or economic discriminations. This explains the fact that Jesus has brought the Good News to Nicodemus, an Israelite doctor, as well as to Zaccheus, a tax collector and leader of the publicans, as well as to Joseph of Arimathea, who was good and just (according to Matthew) and who also awaited the Kingdom of God as a disciple of Jesus.

All these are the poor, in the evangelical sense of the term, for their hearts are "circumcized." Here is a mystery of the heart over which God alone is judge.

We now see that evangelical poverty, this poverty of spirit, holds a central place in the proclamation of the Gospel of the kingdom, but not as a social struggle. It is a spiritual mystery, a detachment of the soul throughout the contingencies and often crucifying events of life. To espouse poverty in this sense does not mean at all to invite militants "to a critical and contentious attack on all the factors within the system which are incompatible with the hope brought by the Gospel."[16] The very opposite is called for: to be critical of oneself, to combat in one's personal life whatever is incompatible with the hope the Gospel offers.

The Social Message of the Gospel

From the preceding it follows that there is, in fact, a social message contained in the Gospel: the most powerful, the most efficacious, the most universal ever transmitted to men. But it can be understood and put into practice only on the condition that we see it in the light of the plan of Christ.

For Christ did not come primarily to renew our society as it exists in history. He came to pay the price of ransom for humanity in spreading God's Kingdom of love to the abyss of suffering and death.

---

[16] *Eglise et Pouvoir*, a document published by the Protestant Federation of France.

In announcing the Kingdom of God, and in establishing it, since his resurrection, in the souls who will receive it, Christ came to restore the human race and to enable those who cooperate with grace to practice, in holiness, the first and second commandments.

The first is:

Hear, O Israel: the Lord thy God is one Lord. Thou shalt love the Lord thy God with all thy heart and with all thy soul and with all thy spirit and with all thy might . . . .

The second is:

Thou shalt love thy neighbor as thyself.

Those who welcome in themselves the Kingdom of God, who are nourished with His body, as he has commanded, and who therefore enjoy the light and the strength necessary to practice His commandments (precepts as well as counsels)—those, indeed, if they are truly poor, if they are truly child-like when they recite together the Our Father—those can truly without affectation, shallow conventionality, or hypocrisy, call one another brothers and sisters.

The social implications of the Gospel appear therefore as a consequence of the interior life of Christ's disciples. Because they die to themselves in peace and joy in order to do God's will each moment, they lovingly renounce themselves in brotherly friendship in order to live in community, to sustain one another in daily life, and especially in trials. Their communal life and, if need be, communal possession of goods is a consequence of their spiritual poverty.

From this point of view the social message of the Gospel is simply the practice, in community life on any scale, of the fraternal charity called for by St. Paul.

Love is always patient and kind; it is never jealous; love is never boastful or conceited; it is never rude or selfish; it does not take offense, and is not resentful. Love takes no pleasure in other people's sins but delights in the truth; it is always ready to excuse, to trust to hope, and to endure whatever comes.

Love does not come to an end. But if there are gifts of prophecy, the time will come when they must fail; or the gift

of languages, it will not continue forever; and knowledge—
for this, too, the time will come when it must fail.[17]

This fraternal life, this life of charity, is essentially a
consequence of the interior life—or, to go further, the mystical
life. Because the original sin transmitted with our human nature is
"each man's own" (according to the teaching recently re-
newed by Paul VI), the social benefits of God's Kingdom can be
realized only through personal mediation, and the active, humble,
and charitable cooperation of each member of the Mystical Body,
of which Christ is the Head.

It is in this sense and to this extent that one can speak of a
social message implied in the Gospel.

It is because Philemon is baptized in Christ that the aging
Paul returns his slave, Onesimus, to him with absolute confidence.
This slave, too, has been baptized by Paul:

> However, I did not want to do anything without your consent;
> it would have been forcing your act of kindness, which should
> be spontaneous. I know you have been deprived of Onesimus
> for a time, but it was only so that you could have him back for
> ever, not as a slave any more, but something much better than a
> slave, a dear brother; especially dear to me, but how much
> more to you, as a blood-brother as well as a brother in the Lord.
> So if all that we have in common means anything to you, wel-
> come him as you would me; . . . [18]

It is obvious that juridical, social, and economic conditions,
being just, favor brotherhood in Christ more than others. We shall
return to this later. But if a man does not *first* change in his heart, no
mere reform of a structure or system will ever solve social problems.
In any case, such a reform, presented as the essence of the Gospel,
though dissociated from it in practice, would not bring about what
we have seen to be the heart of the message of Christ: spiritual
poverty which yields everything to God; the adoptive sonship which
makes communion with our brothers possible.

---

[17] I. Corinthians 13:4-8.
[18] Philemon 14-17.

2

AN AMBIGUOUS
LIBERATION

*Is the welding of Christ's Gospel
with the call to revolution compatible or
incompatible with what we know to be Christian faith?*

For the last two hundred years, the cry of Rousseau, at the beginning of his *Social Contract*, has resounded in the ears of every generation: "Man is born free; yet everywhere he is in chains."[1] The commentary that follows is no less eloquent: "To renounce one's freedom is to renounce one's quality as a human being, the rights of humanity, and even one's duties."[2] The consequence is clear: "As long as a people is forced to obey, and it obeys, it does well, as soon as it can shake this yoke, and it shakes it, it does something better."[3]

This vague desire for a condition which he calls liberty has always been deeply rooted in men's hearts. It is already dealt with at the very beginning of Genesis. Ancient history is marked

---

[1] J. J. Rousseau, *Complete Works*, Vol. VI (Editions Dalibon, 1824), p. 4.
[2] *Ibid.*, p. 12.
[3] *Ibid.*, p. 4.

out by alternating narratives of bondage and liberation, be it of whole peoples or of individual slaves.

In the course of the Christian centuries, one usually spoke of liberties in the plural. They were frequently called franchises, and pertained both to the state of persons and the usage of goods.

Individualistic Liberation

It was the individualistic revolution of 1789 which, under the influence of Rousseau and the Encyclopedists, made an idol of abstractly defined liberty, and acclaimed it as an essential precondition for any truly human life. This liberty meant absolute autonomy of the individual, whereby he would no longer be bound by natural law, nor by political, economic, or social bonds, which can also be considered natural. In personal decisions, self-interest could legitimately replace justice. In social relationships, contracts freely entered into must replace the law or professional regulation. It is in this absolute separation from his bonds that man, who is innately good, would cease to be corrupted by society.

The economic system resulting from this unlimited individual freedom was to disappoint the hopes of its founders. In abolishing the right of association, whether of the employers, or of the wage-earners, or of both united, the revolutionary legislation, which spread throughout the Christian West, abolished, in fact, all the guarantees and protections upon which society had previously rested.

Individual laborers were at the mercy of individual holders of capital. The former could no longer rely on the moral uprightness of their employers; neither could they defend themselves through the moral strength of rights (which had been at times complex, but carefully elaborated within trade corporations). Nor could they defend themselves by the sheer physical strength of numbers, since, according to the Le Chapelier law, "the annihilation" of any and all kinds of association "of the citizens who share the same profession" was one of the fundamental bases of the French constitution.[4]

Pope Pius VI did not wait for this law to be passed before in-

---

[4] Le Chapelier Law of June 17, 1791, Article I.

tervening in an attempt to safeguard the rights of God and man. On March 10, 1791, in a letter, *Quod Aliquantum,* addressed to Cardinal de la Rochefoucauld and the other bishops of the National Assembly, he had raised his voice against the civil constitution of the clergy and its inevitable consequences.

> The necessary consequence of the constitution decreed by the assembly is to annihilate the Catholic religion.

And he gives the reason:

> What could have been more senseless than the establishment among men of that unbridled equality and liberty which seem to choke reason—the most precious gift Nature has bestowed upon man—and the only one that clearly distinguishes him from animals? After having created man and having placed him in a garden of delights did not God threaten man with death if he ate of the fruit of the tree of knowledge of good and evil? When, later, man's disobedience had made him guilty, did He not impose new obligations on him through the voice of Moses? And even though He had given man the power through free will to determine himself for good or evil, did he not surround man with precepts and commandments that could save him if man chose to fulfill them?[5]

As we can see, those who reproach the Church for having waited until 1891, with the publication of the encyclical of Leo XIII, to condemn liberalism, are misinformed. It was in 1791—one hundred years earlier—that the Supreme Pontiff warned the French bishops about the religious and social danger concealed in the worship of "Liberty" whose idolatrous cult was not to delay long before claiming first the blood of the guillotine victims and then, throughout the nineteenth century, the unrestrained exploitation of workers, men, women and children, caught defenseless under the power of money, the only remaining source of freedom in an economic world that had been dechristianized.

Socialist Liberation

The nineteenth century socialists, claiming the same absolute freedom, strayed in another direction, though this time more egali-

---

[5] A. F. Utz, *The Social Doctrine of the Church,* Vol. III, p. 2519.

tarian, and conceived a utopia which would no longer allow the horrors of the exploitation of man by man which Manchesterian liberalism had engendered.

Like the liberals, they rejected as a social principle the idea that man is subject to moral precepts and natural bonds. They substituted for this the image of a man radically autonomous in his conscience but defined collectively, and striving to create a society in which the equality of all men would not be jeopardized by universal freedom.

Proudhon's Socialism

Still more than Fourier and Saint Simon, Proudhon opens the way. He perceives the problem clearly: the individual entering into a group encounters opposition. Should he submit himself to the collectivity and become a mere organ? No, retorts Proudhon, who published three large volumes on *Justice in Revolution and in the Church*. He attempts to set revolution in opposition to revelation and endeavors to show that the Church recognizes only a sinful and cowardly humanity, whose salvation can only come from the will of another—the will of God. Proudhon contrasts the socialist revolution to this image and puts forth a theory of liberty and justice in equality. To the system of subordination of services advocated by the Church, he opposes equality of services. To the moral right of political authority to rule, he opposes the impersonal, invisible, anonymous social power. This results from the commutative action of economic forces and industrial groups, action which is the very incarnation of liberty itself. The revolution, while constantly organizing and reestablishing equality, guarantees each man a plenitude of life. While establishing justice in the state, it insures universal communion. The organ of collective reason is like the organ of collective strength. Proudhon claims that this organ is found in the group, i.e. in every group of men formed for the discussion of ideas and the pursuit of the right. In following these guidelines, Proudhon predicts that socialism will be put into practice, and thus the sanctification of humanity by itself.

Proudhon sets revelation and revolution in opposition. Yet, upon fulfillment of certain conditions he is ready to take the Church as an ally. Let her agree to preach a revolutionary morality to the sovereign people in her churches; let her abolish whatever is theological and ecclesiastical; let her relinquish all her possessions to the commune; let her release all monks and priests from their perpetual vows—in short, let her "desacralize" herself, and do away with the clergy; let her preach the revolution, and her own salvation will be assured!

In order to clarify his own conception of the total liberation of man, Proudhon exclaims, "What could this adoration of a Supreme Being be, if not a representation of justice, i.e., of a respect for humanity? . . . What are these divine Trinities we see revealed in all mythologies, if not the first categorization of the human soul both individual and collective? . . . Are not your angels these collective powers which economics reveals to us? . . . Is not grace this faculty for perceiving the ideal with which nature has endowed us to serve as a perpetual incitement to justice? Your sacraments, the initiation of the family and society? Your original sin, a parable of the state of nature, from which civilization daily liberates us? . . . your resurrection, the ceaseless reviving of the species?[6]

Upon meditating these texts, one cannot help but perceive a proudhonian flavor in the very core of the events which have followed the Council of Vatican II. This is especially true if one notes Proudhon's fervor when addressing Msgr. Mathieu, then Archbishop of Besançon, at the close of his work: "I am just as religious as you are and almost in the same terms. I shall do more. To celebrate this memorable union . . . we shall prostrate ourselves at your feet." To which Msgr. Mathieu answered, "Proudhon is not an atheist; he is an enemy of God."

Such is the "religious" socialism of Proudhon. He relies on the worldwide proclamation of justice to take the place of God among the working communities. These would come closer and closer to equality by reciprocity of services, performed without human subordination.

---

[6] Proudhon, *La Justice dans la Révolution et dans l' Eglise,* Tome III, pp. 602-603.

Marxist Socialism

The preceding secures Proudhon the title of "petit bourgeois," granted him by Karl Marx, who interprets these dreams as reactionary and utopian socialism.

The liberation of man to which both Marx's work and the practice of Lenin's dialectics give concrete scope is directed toward a different goal. It does not dream of transforming man and freeing him from all subordination through a moral teaching. It aims at abolishing the capitalistic mode of production based on private property, which, it claims, is the historical cause of the antagonism between the classes and of the exploitation of man by man. For Marx, this "economic alienation" lies at the root of men's need for the consolation they seek in faith; thus he terms it the "religious alienation." The realization of economic liberation through socialism necessarily implies working toward liberation from all religion.

Like Rousseau and Proudhon, Marx considers a revolution to be the precondition for the liberated state. Rousseau places all his hope in the "general will" of the sovereign people, Proudhon in "justice." Marx places his hope in the "proletariat." However, the period of its established dictatorship will be transitory. For it will result in the abolition of all classes and the creation of the classless society.

The Church has made many responses to these socialist and communist systems—already in 1846 with the encyclical, *Qui Pluribus*; then led by Leo XIII with the encyclical *Rerum Novarum* in 1891, which exposed the connection existing between liberalism and socialism; and then again by Pius XI in *Miserentissimus Redemptor* in 1928, *Quadragesimo anno* in 1931, and *Divini Redemptoris* in 1937. The common doctrine of Catholic teaching is expressed in the teaching of Leo XIII: "Man must remain completely in a real and ceaseless dependence on God and therefore, it is absolutely impossible to understand man's freedom without his duty of obedience to God, the submission to His will."[7]

---

[7] *Libertas praetantissimum*, in Utz. loc. cit., Tome I, p. 213.

The question Christians must raise after Proudhon is whether the kind of equality which repudiates every human hierarchy is or is not willed by God. The question they must pose after Marx and Lenin is whether the right to private property—even of the means of production—is in accordance with God's will and whether the latter (i.e., the will of God) has truly settled the question of whether man is prior to society.

The popes, especially Leo XIII and John XXIII, have answered all these questions in explicit and thorough documents concerning the social doctrine of the Church—teaching from which Pope Paul VI invited Catholics to draw "principles of refutation, norms of judgment and directives for action."[8]

Complete Liberation

Step by step the liberation which, in the eighteenth century meant individualistic democracy and in the nineteenth, socialistic egalitarianism, has expanded its field of application. The works of Freud have given the notion of liberation a new aspect: they teach man to liberate himself from sexual repressions which would lie at the root of his fears and failures. As Marx wanted to destroy religious alienation through the abolition of capitalistic property, Freud deems religion to be a collective neurosis which psychoanalysis has the mission to help break down. Taking these works as a point of departure, Wilhelm Reich goes further in proclaiming the necessity for a sexual revolution capable of establishing "a revolutionary morality" of sexual drives, freeing man from capitalistic morality, the repressive morality of the dominating class.[9]

In line with this sexual revolution, seen as the pivot of a cultural revolution, we must mention the claims which agitate public opinion today. In the name of the total liberation of man, the widespread use of contraception, the right to free abortion, and the right to trial-marriage have successively been demanded, as well as the right of persons who "after having known several types of

---

[8] Pope Paul VI, *Octogesima adveniens*, no. 4.

[9] Cf. Wilhelm Reich, *The Sexual Revolution* Ed. Plon. p. 35.

41

sexual experiences, have chosen homosexuality as their preferred mode of activity."[10]

Indeed, these are not marginal demands. They are ultimately linked to the overall movement whose goal is total liberation. In progressive stages they reveal man's and woman's denial of what they are. Marriage itself must be abolished. "If independence is a necessary concomitant of freedom, women must not marry."[11] And Kate Millet adds: "It may be that a second wave of the sexual revolution might at last accomplish its aim of freeing half the race from its immemorial subordination."[12] Similarly, a magazine interviewer recently did not hesitate to conclude, after having interrogated a number of persons, "Truly, it is unjust to be born a woman."[13]

Such, in its complex impetus, is the scope of the complete liberation of man. Rousseau dreamed of a political, Marx of an economic, and Freud of a sexual liberation. All of them (but each in his own way) attack religion, which they see to be concomitant with personal authority in politics, private property in economics, and sexual morality in conjugal love and in the family. We may state it thus: the evolution of these doctrines is reaching its end. Though they were opposed to each other a short time ago, they now tend to commingle in a system, not only among the theoreticians, but also in a collective mentality which is gaining force. The system may be multiform, but in its basic inspiration it is unified: the rejection of human nature defined as dependent on an order established by the Creator in the physical, moral, personal and social structure of man.

We do not make this assertion gratuitously, nor on our own account. It has been formulated by the clearest and strictest thinkers of the revolution. It was expressed already by Rousseau: "He who dares attempt to found a people must feel himself capable, so to speak, of changing human nature."[14] With Marx, the question is

---

[10] *Teach-in on Sexuality,* University of Montréal, Editions ed l'Homme.

[11] Germaine Greer, *The Female Eunuch* (New York: McGraw Hill, 1971), p. 318.

[12] Kate Millet, *Sexual Politics* (New York: Doubleday, 1970), p. 363.

[13] *Le Journal du Dimanche,* January 30, 1972, p. 22.

[14] J. J. Rousseau, *loc. cit.,* p. 55.

no longer even one of changing human nature; it is to be recreated. It is the Collective Man who "creates" himself throughout history. "For the Socialist Man, so-called world history is nothing other than the creation of man through human work."[15]

It must be stressed that this is the source of inspiration for Freud, Reich, and Marcuse. The latter touches on the very heart of the problem. He blames man's incapacity to attain beatitude *in time*. "The idea of integral human liberation therefore necessarily contains the vision of the struggle against time . . . . But the fatal enemy of lasting gratification is TIME, the inner finiteness."[16]

In a special issue of "Modern Times," Claude Lanzman affirms the same thought, no longer in terms of internal finitude, i.e., of beatitude, but rather in terms of finality. "The negative movement initiated by the left is a constructive one. A refusal is incarnated completely only through the creation of a new reality. In transcending the limits the world imposes on us, man conquers both the world and himself. This conquest is an invention which can be neither defined nor limited by any rule. From the very moment when man has taken the step to illegitimacy, when he has accepted his contingency, man reveals himself as possessing absolute autonomy. *His will has become his raison d'être.* There is no question of his rejoining a realm whose goals are given. There is no end for man higher than he is himself; there is no other end for man than man, himself. Man is his own end."[17]

This is probably the most radical sign of the total liberation of man. For Rousseau, what matters is to change human nature. For Marx, the key question is the creation of man through human work. Marcuse aims at conquering human finitude; Lanzman affirms that man is his own end.

This is the cult of *man*. He appears as the Alpha and Omega. The liberation at stake here is, most explicitly, not a social but an ontological liberation. Man aims at the transformation of society

[15] J. Y. Calvez, *La Pensée de Karl Marx*, ed. du Suril, pp. 301, s. 99.

[16] Herbert Marcuse, *Eros and Civilization* (Boston: Beacon Press, 1955), p. 191.

[17] *Les Temps Modernes*, No. 112-113, May 1955, p. 1650.

because he longs to change human nature. He wishes to abolish human subordination in political society, in social economy and in family life because it reflects and expresses man's ontological dependence on God.

The Social Doctrine of the Church

In the context of this kind of contemporary thought we are better equipped to understand the admonition of Paul VI in *Octogesima Adveniens*, to draw our principles of reflection, norms of judgment and directives for action from the encyclicals and other documents of the common magisterium which constitutes the authentic social doctrine of the Church. For this doctrine is not simply deduced from the Gospels, as it is taken by the defenders of morality properly understood, and who seek in revelation and theological discourses the complete foundations for the moral and social order.

The institution of a temporal order is not the aim of the liberation Christ brought us. Therefore, neither is that the nature of the social message for today contained in the Gospel. This has already been made clear.

For this reason also, such is not the enduring and explicit teaching of the Sovereign Pontiffs. This is powerfully expressed by Pope Pius XII in his summary on natural law. This is the foundation upon which the social doctrine of the Church rests. It is precisely her Christian conception of the world which has both inspired and sustained the Church in the elaboration of this doctrine on such a basis. Healthy human nature can accomplish much, provided it opens itself to the total contribution of the Christian faith. It can save man from the grasp of technocracy and materialism.[18]

To affirm that the social doctrine of the Church is based on natural law does not mean to secularize it. For this doctrine is supernatural, *not* because the Gospel invites us to build a new society stripped of social hierarchy, private property, parental and con-

---

[18] Pius XII, Allocution to the Members of a Congress on Humanistic Studies, September 25, 1949.

jugal ties, but because through grace man is divinized in himself, his virtues are infused, his acts can merit eternal life. Furthermore, it is the supernatural elevation of the person through divine grace that will enable him to live in a new way, in marriage and family life, in the management of private goods, and under the authority of the various political hierarchies. If faithful to this teaching, he can become more upright, humanly speaking, more just, more fraternal.

As if he already foresaw the kind of self-destruction which since Paul VI has been explicitly deplored, Pius XII warned that "The Enemy of Christ . . . does and has done everything in his power to spread erroneous ideas about man and the world, about history, the structure of society, and the sphere of economics."[19] He specified further the teaching of the Church: "We reject communism *as a social system*, virtue of Christian doctrine and we must affirm, in particular, the foundations of natural law."[20]

The total liberation of man attacks marriage and family in the name of sexual freedom, the state in the name of individual dignity, private property in the name of social justice. In fact it is the dignity of the person as the image of God which suffers from this "liberation." For marriage and the family, the state, and private property tend by their very nature to form and develop man as a person, to protect him and to enable him to contribute through his own free collaboration and personal responsibility to the upholding and development—also personal—of social life.[21]

Three Meanings of the Word "Liberation"

From the preceding, it should be clear that the word liberation is used today in three different senses:

1. *First Meaning: the spiritual liberation of the Gospel*

Liberation here signifies the liberation of man through Jesus

---

[19] Pius XII, Allocution of May 1, 1955.
[20] Pius XII, Radiophonic Message, Dec. 24, 1955.
[21] Pius XII, Radiophonic Message, Dec. 24, 1953.

45

Christ. It is the redemption of humanity that is in question. The liberation in the Old Testament are only figurative similes intended to direct man from a temporal understanding of political liberation (of one people subjected to another), to the spiritual understanding of the liberation from sin. The notions of liberation and justice in the Epistle to the Romans has nothing ambiguous about it: "You were once slaves of sin, but thank God you submitted without reservation to the creed you were taught. You may have been freed from the slavery of sin, but only to become 'slaves' of righteousness."[22] This liberation is, in itself, independent of an temporal condition. The slave himself benefits from it, even if he is not freed. He is one made free by the Lord, and this belongs to another order. The voluntary, free poverty which this liberation brings about is a detachment of the soul. It is not a revolt against economic poverty, a class struggle, or a sexual subversion.

2. Second Meaning: Natural Liberation

Liberation can also designate the Christian realization of the social doctrine founded on natural rights in temporal life. Indeed, the Gospel contains an explicit social message: the second commandment makes fraternal love in God's grace the social bond uniting communities in Christ.

What, then, is the order which God the Creator has inscribed on the personal and social nature of man, and which the Christian is called upon to restore each moment in cooperation with baptismal grace?

This order is not directly given in revelation, though both the Old and the New Testaments refer to it; but we shall have to return to this later. God's respect for man is such that He has wanted him to discover for himself, as far as this is possible through his own activity, whatever reason, enlightened by grace, is capable of understanding and formulating. Thus the revelation of the Decalogue to the Jews through Moses did not prevent the development among the pagans of man's understanding of unwritten laws, of a natural law. It is to Aristotle's glory to have formulated

---

[22] Romans 6:17-18.

its first synthesis. This, imperfect as it may have been, has served no less than the Decalogue as a basis for the commentaries of the Common Doctor and for the social and moral teaching of the Church.

Thus we see that natural law, received in grace, creates the foundation for social liberation. This has been the teaching of all the popes. "No believer," Paul VI teaches us, "will wish to deny that the teaching authority of the Church is competent to interpret even the natural moral law."[23] This liberation requires a respect for institutions of natural law, the moral uprightness of the spouses between themselves, of parents and children, of the governing and the governed, of employers and employees, that leads to the permanent dynamism of justice founded on the personal responsibility of each man and woman, the subject and foundation of moral life.

Such a liberation hangs in delicate balance. It does not exclude sin, nor the social consequences of sin. It does not exempt one from carrying the cross which is a result of the sins of all men. It rests on the trust granted to each man that, with the help of grace, he can perfect himself, practice mercy, and put his whole hope in the beatific vision, not in an earthly city.

3. Third Meaning: Revolutionary Liberation

Finally, liberation can be understood, as it is commonly understood today, as the denial of natural law, the acceptance of the thesis of the total liberation of human society through the destruction of the complementary duality of man and woman (by abolition of marriage); of parents and children (by abolition of the family); of employer and employee (by abolition of private property); and even of the governing and the governed (by abolition of the state). In this sense, it would be held that the redemption through Jesus Christ and the infusion of grace in human nature, far from being a guiding light and a source of the strength required to be a good spouse, a good father, a good head of state or a good employer, is, in fact, liberation from all social structures founded on natural law.

---

[23] Pope Paul VI, *Humanae Vitae*, no. 4.

47

From that point on, the true meaning of the redemption of Jesus Christ, at least for the man of our era, would be the mutation of nature through a revolution modifying the structures and mechanisms in a way that has been geared to prevent man from falling victim any longer to the sins of men. This is the thesis of those who believe that God's grace has been given to man not only that he might, through the power of love, avoid sinning, be forgiven for his sins, or forgive the offenses he has suffered from others, but rather, from now on, in order to suffer no longer from others' sins.

In short, liberation in the contemporary social and intellectual context, because of its evangelical, moral and revolutionary ambiguity, can mean:

(1) spiritual liberation from sin through Jesus Christ;

(2) temporal liberation through Christian life, with respect for natural law;

(3) liberation from the limits and ends assigned by God to human nature, giving this ontological revolt the name of redemption.

It should be clear that only the first two meanings are in agreement with the social message contained in the Gospel. The third meaning is opposed to it. It is well known that the ambiguity of these three different definitions is used by revolutionaries in order to confuse Christians. So, for instance, in an interview with Georges Marchais published in *The Cross* and handed out afterwards in hundreds of thousands of copies at the doors of churches, under cover of the authority enjoyed by this paper, the adjunct general secretary of the French Communist Party hides the link which exists between natural law and the social teaching of the Church. He declares: "The building of a socialist society does not presuppose the universal acceptance of materialism. It presupposes something completely different: the transfer of the property of all great means of production and exchange to the state, and the exercise of power by the workers, the popular masses. Is anything in the Christian faith opposed to this? I do not believe so."[24]

This is a crucial statement. Not only the temporal fate of our

---

[24] *La Croix*, November 19, 1970.

Western civilization, but the very orthodoxy of faith is at stake. Can the Gospel in itself be considered a social message of charity capable of being adapted to and lived in any and every system of government, regardless of whether or not it respects the dignity of the person? In particular, can it be adapted to and lived in any and every system of government, regardless of whether or not it respects the dignity of the person? In particular, can it be adapted to and lived in the framework of economic socialism, meaning collectivity of goods; a cultural socialism, meaning a classless society; a state socialism, meaning abolition of the state; a sexual socialism, meaning destruction of the family? Does the Gospel call for the creation of structures that would completely and forever abolish the possibility that man may suffer from the sins of man? Let us not assume that these things are unrelated: communism of goods and sexual communism call for one another, from Plato to the sexual revolution. "Marriage would constitute a group formation within the commune and would further impair the unity of the commune."[25]

Has the Gospel from its beginning been rightly presented by the ordinary magisterium as implying a natural moral law, a natural social law, the elements of which are organically unified, and the continuous reestablishment of which is an intrinsic part of the temporal mission of the Christian? Or shall we say that the popes who taught it, including Pope Paul VI—who, in following his predecessors, is teaching it in *Humanae Vitae*—are mistaken? Are they misleading us? Or do the opponents of the Pope intend to make us renounce the teaching of the Church?

Can one live in a state of grace and militantly denounce every non-socialist government as an element of "established disorder"? Can one live in a state of grace and fight for the pill, collective marriages and the pastoral of homosexuals?

The major anomaly of the synodal document on *Justice in the World* lies in the fact that it abounds in *external* denunciations of objective injustices without appealing, as both Christian morality and natural law demand, to the spiritual reform of those who are

---

[25] Wilhelm Reich, *Sexual Revolution*, Farrar - Straus - Giroux. New York 1971. p. 227

49

socially, economically and politically responsible. It places its hope, not in man's accomplished redemption, but rather in a "fight for justice" and a "transformation of the world." In view of the quotations we have cited here it cannot be denied that this document is based on a dangerous equivocation. This is particularly true when it states that this fight and participation in it "appear as a completely essential dimension of the preaching of the Gospel, which is the Church's mission for the redemption of humanity *and its liberation from any and every oppressive situation.*"[26]

This can be interpreted to mean that the notion of natural law is implicit in the Gospel—if one admits the existence of natural law, and that it is implied in the Gospel. But if one refuses to admit this, it can just as easily be interpreted to mean that the Gospel message implies total revolution, the mutation of human nature, the genesis of the independent man whose only purpose is that which he creates for himself, and whose self becomes the object of his own homage.

Voted on in a fragmentary way by bishops preoccupied with the question of clerical celibacy, and in a climate of social preoccupation, the synodal document on justice in the world poses, as we see, weighty problems in view of the prevalent trends of our society.

According to the teaching of Paul VI, these problems must be solved by referring to the social doctrine of the Church and its foundation: natural law. Failure to do so will bring us close to a state which the apostle admonishes us to avoid: "Do not harness yourselves in an uneven team with unbelievers. Virtue is no companion for crime. Light and darkness have nothing in common. Christ is not the ally of Belial, nor has a believer anything to share with an unbeliever."[27]

Justice in this world can never be the application of the grace of redemption to a humanity which rejects the Cross and revolts against its own nature and the duties inscribed therein.

---

[26] Synodal Document, Introduction, *The Cross (La Croix)*, Dec. 14, 1971, p. 8. (Italics mine.)

[27] II Corinthians 6:14.

3

The "Revolutionary" Gospel

A Few Examples
Five features of the phenomenon of
coupling the Gospel and revolution

What are the various meanings of the word liberation in the contemporary intellectual and social context? Which are in agreement with the social message implied in the Gospel and which are opposed to it?

Every day articles, pamphlets, meetings of laymen and militant priests work toward the reindoctrination of the minds of Catholics and Protestants, training them never to think "Gospel" without thinking of the ambiguous phrase, "liberation of man." Are they speaking of spiritual liberation? Of course! But at the same time, and as if the two concepts are linked by necessity, the temporal liberation of the socialist or communist brand. In the final analysis, we are being presented with a revolutionary Gospel in which these two concepts are inseparably intertwined.

The publication of the synodal document referred to in the introduction was followed in close succession by the appearance of articles, studies, questionnaires, all stamped with this same character.

51

Some Examples

In a recent 1972 issue of *Illustrated Catholic Life*, the Rev. M. D. Bouyer, O. P., entitled a commentary he made on the Gospel, "A Dangerous Jesus." This title was not chosen in order to arouse fear. It was chosen in order that Catholic readers might be assured that they are in line with faith if they imitate Jesus on this point: to become dangerous themselves.

The author writes, "Jesus speaks and acts as controversialist .... He openly distinguishes himself from all those whose profession, public image, or power consist in their living the law of Moses. They capitalize on it to their own advantage, making it their own property, in order later to market it to the people."[1]

The whole article is written in this vein. It suggests that Jesus was concerned not with sin, but with social classes. There is an unresolvable ambiguity underlying these statements which equate the spiritual liberation brought by Jesus Christ and the suggestive words and images which invite the reader to believe that the salvation of his soul is linked to the abolition of capitalism, of private property, of the power of the state, and to the establishment of the classless society.

In the December 31, 1971 issue of the magazine for scout and guide leaders in France,[2] a long poem appeared by Marie Thérèse Cheroutre, Jean Debruyne and Emile X. Visseaux, printed in large characters on a double page. According to the introduction the poem was the fruit of national camps, meetings between laymen and priests of the departmental teams, which had taken place in the course of the previous summer. "The revolution which it proclaims is that of the Gospel," it is claimed. We shall limit ourselves to the quotation of a few passages with the assurance that they convey an adequate idea of the whole.

The scouting we propose is a choice.
Today, to educate is to transform the world.
Man is our first word

---

[1] *Illustrated Catholic Life*, February 9-15, 1972, pp. 26-27.
[2] "Jeunes en marche" (*Youth in Action*), 125, boulevard St. Denis 92 Courbevoie, n. 25.

For we live with the younger ones in the concreteness of the
days.
And the patient march which makes man grow,
We must begin within ourselves,
To reconcile man with his dignity.
We are far away; we must follow our choices to the end.

Without commenting in detail upon this beginning, we can simply take note of the passage referring to the promethean definition of education: " . . . to educate is to transform the world," paraphrasing the sentence of St. John, "In the beginning was the Word . . . and the Word was God." It now becomes, "Man is our first word." And this revolutionary Gospel speaks of "reconciling man with his dignity." Should not the reconciliation rather be with God?

The second verse juxtaposes to the first a sort of Christ at the service of human aims:

It is today that Christ liberates us.
A revolution ceaselessly changes our hearts.
Jesus Christ comes to open up for us all man's possibilities,
Hope is not dead if we will witness to this.
etc.

The third verse deserves to be quoted in its entirety, for it unmasks the revolutionary aim discreetly contained in this "poem":

Let us create a new vision of scouting.
Our scouting cannot accommodate itself
To a world that refuses to change anything.
Our scouting cannot become accomplice
To a world that imprisons man in contempt.
We can no longer allow our future
To be determined by objects.
Jesus Christ makes us, too, capable of wrath and indignation.
He makes us contemporary with the beatitudes.
Each time a child learns to pass judgment upon the world
And to recognize himself in his own deeds.
We win the bet we made on man
And a liberty which escapes profit.

This polemic against "a world which refuses to change anything," then against "a world which imprisons man in contempt," is preparation for the Marxist terminology of "objects which choose our future" (as if our future were purely temporal and essentially determined by historical materialism, and not by our sins and virtues). Like Father M. D. Bouyer, who invites his readers to imitate a belligerent and dangerous Christ, the poem claims that Christ makes us capable of wrath and indignation, a statement immediately balanced by the reference to the beatitudes. The last verse leads the reader to the conclusion that the spiritual liberation brought by Jesus Christ implies a society "without profit," i.e., without property. This is a precondition of the liberation.

What *Catholic Life* is teaching its readers, and the Scouts of France their leaders, was contemplated by the Movement of the Lay Apostolate, united by a liaison team of laymen, on February 12, 1972. Their goal was to coordinate an international movement "to regionalize and decentralize research," "to promote a dialogue," "to bring about confrontations," and so forth. The subject of this vast collective meditation in which offices, organizations, priests, militants, and the various commissions unite to plan the future implies the same ambiguous welding of two themes: "Liberation of men and salvation in Jesus Christ." The following is the text submitted to all those concerned for meditation:

What Liberation?

In your daily life—professional or school work, family, walk of life, etc.—do you perceive in yourself and in others a longing for liberation?

Do you prefer to talk about "salvation" or "promotion" of men? or about "development"? or about "solidarity"? or about "the common good"? or "reconciliation"?

From what or whom are you to save and liberate yourself? From things that crush you? From people who oppress you? From yourself?

How are we to bring about this liberation? Is it a question of transformation of hearts? of politics? of class struggle? of patience? of violence?

What Faith in What God?

What is your faith? Is it a matter of course that it liberates you? Does it have an impact on your life and your action? Do your life and action work against it? Is your faith linked to an ideology? to a political project? Can it be reduced to this? Can it do without it?

Who is this Christ who is called savior and liberator? In what sense does his Word liberate us and in what sense does it not? In what sense can one say that his life, his death, and what his disciples call his resurrection are (or are not) a message of deliverance?

How do you discern the countenance of God through the words and action of Jesus? How does God speak to us of liberation? through whom and what? Should we "liberate" our faith? How?

Does the desire to work for the liberation of men in Jesus Christ call the Christian to specific political choices? In this sense, can there be a pluralism among Christians?

Which Church?

Do you think that the Church today is a sign of liberation? Who is the Church?

Is there a need of a Church to announce the liberation of men in Jesus Christ? If yes, of what Church?

Does the Church, in so far as it is a gathering of Christians, have a duty to take a public stand to pronounce the word of liberation?

Should the Church, herself be liberated? If so, how?

I shall not undertake to comment on this questionnaire in detail. No one can deny that it is constructed so as to bring about strong intellectual associations between two series of words: salvation (pertaining to eternal life) and promotion (referring to temporal promotion). The notion of liberation never implies specifically the liberation from the influence of wicked angels, or from sin, but only from "things," from "people," even from oneself. The questions related to faith accentuate this illegitimate welding together of two concepts: "Is your faith linked to an ideology?"

We should also take note of the amalgamation in the second series of questions where those of a purely spiritual nature ("Who is Jesus?" "What countenance of God . . .") are closely followed by a question like, "Does the liberation of men in Jesus Christ call Christians to specific political choices?" As for the third series of questions, it advances perceptibly a step further: "Is there a need of a

Church to announce the liberation of men through Jesus Christ? . . .
In so far as it is a gathering of Christians, does the Church have the
duty to take a public stand to pronounce a word of liberation?"

It is not said what word . . . . But the last question anticipates
the case of those who would disagree with that particular word: the
Church herself would in that case have to be liberated!

One could object that this is nothing more than a questionnaire,
that the participants are given full freedom to answer it, to criticize
it. The fact remains that the questions, their implications, their
progression reveal an intent, a trend; and in the final analysis, in this
type of questionnaire it is the questions posed which, through their
wording and progression, are most decisive. For those who refuse to
participate and withdraw are, *ipso facto* disqualified. They are designated as those "who do not want any change."

What *Catholic Life* suggests to its readers, the scouts of France
to their leaders, the movements and organizations of the lay
apostolate to their lay and ecclesiastical members, has been discussed more explicitly in a document entitled, *Justice and Development in a Parisian District*, by a commission called Justice in Paris.[3]

The questionnaire addressed to the movements of the lay
apostolate asks, "How is liberation to be accomplished? Is it a
matter of transformation of hearts? of politics? of class struggle? of
patience? of violence?" The document, *Justice in Paris*, gives
an answer and intends "to unmask the idealistic and subject
illusion according to which it suffices to transform man's heart in
order for these problems to be solved." This same document,
while affirming as early as its first section that "the proper mission
confided to the Church by Christ is not of an economic or social
order," nonetheless completely remains in line with all the preceding statements. It affirms that "the Church as such, and at all
levels, must be a force of controversy." "The work of salvation
through Christ" is defined as:

(1) the respect of the person and groups of persons,
(2) the work of liberation,

---

[3] In *Presence et Dialogue de Paris*, 30, rue Barbet-de-Jouy, Paris VII. See also
the article signed F. L. in *La Croix*, February 6, 1972, under the title,
"Christians are Preoccupied about Justice in Paris."

(3) the goal of reconciliation and recapitulation.

All these aims must, of course, be pursued "in the sense of a human becoming which finds its ultimate meaning only in the eschatological vision of the kingdom."

Meditation on the whole of this document cannot be strongly enough recommended. It provides us, if not with the answers, at least with the principles upon which are based the answers to the questionnaire spread in and through the movements and organizations for the lay apostolate. Is this the result of chance?

I could easily multiply references of this type. This would lead us to examine the interview granted by Jacques Duclos to the *Croix-Dimanche du Nord*,[4] and the commentary by Claude Beaufort published in this same weekly. It would also lead us to comment upon a letter of Don Helder Camara, written in preparation for the April 1972 meeting of Driebergen, and treating, among other things, banking and real estate structures. This would also require the analysis of two parallel books, published almost simultaneously: *The Left of Christ*,[5] by Jacques Duchesne, which bears the subtitle, "Can one reconcile Marx and Jesus?," and *The Marxists and World Evolution*,[6] signed by three members of the Communist Party, which answers the question, "Can one be a Communist and a Catholic?"

We would also be called upon to refute the way in which Ph. Roqueplo devotes an article in *L'Esprit* of November 1971 to binding together salvation and liberation under the general title, "Reinvent the Church!" We should also take note of the fact that the theme of justice has been selected by a good many parishes as a topic of lenten sermons with the idea that "the place of Easter in the Church is her involvement in the service of justice in the world."

But we are not taking an inventory. It is enough for us to ascertain that the religious investigator who follows the current scene cannot avoid being, so to speak, "apostrophized" by the obvi-

---

[4] *La Croix du Nord*, no. 172, February 6, 1972.

[5] Jacques Duquesne, *The Left of Christ*, Editions Grasset.

[6] Roland Leroy, Casanova, et al., *The Marxists and the Evolution of the Catholic World*, Editions Sociales.

ous technique with which the welding of eternal salvation to temporal liberation has taken place in Christian opinion in the first months of 1972.

Five Features of this False Coupling

This coupling of temporal liberation with eternal salvation, which we have been able to verify through the preceding texts, exhibits the following characteristics:

1. *It is planned.* All of a sudden a particular Catholic and Protestant press, the various lay apostolic movements, the offices, and the books offer to—or rather impose upon—Christians, for meditation in various forms, the double-sided concept of "eternal salvation-temporal liberation."

2. *It is devoid of doctrinal foundation.* "The struggle for justice and for the participation in the transformation of the world (appears to us) as a fully constitutive dimension of the teaching of the Gospel, which is the Church's mission for the redemption of humanity and its liberation from any and every oppressive situation." This claim, from the synodal document, is a theological opinion which, even if affirmed by synodal vote, raises problems.

3. *It is ambiguous.* The persistent juxtaposition of the words, "preaching," "mission," "redemption," "salvation," "eschatological vision," and so forth with the words, "work of liberation," "struggle for justice," "liberation from any and every oppressive situation," or "total liberation of man," brings about a lasting confusion of the three possible meanings of the word liberation. The corruption of the language brings about the corruption of understanding, including the understanding of faith.

4. *It does not define; it insinuates.* This is one of the common features of all the texts I have quoted. One of them skims the question in discussing the transformation of man's heart as being "an idealistic illusion" on the social plane; another brings out the possibility of "public positions" of the Church "to speak a word of liberation." The third speaks of "a freedom from profit," the fourth of those "who capitalize on their power to their own profit," the fifth suggests the condemnation of a "mentality which beatifies possession." But all this is furtive, preparatory.

No one today says clearly and distinctly, "The Gospel is incompatible today with the private possession of the means of production." This is effected in a more subtle way: whether through ambiguities, intellectual atmospheres, or misleading hints, we are led to believe that the system of private property labors under an evangelical condemnation. Although this is never unequivocally stated, it has a cumulative influence and weighs on the mind.

5. *It exercises a moral violence.* It is always in the name of the Gospel that this campaign is spread and deepened. It is also carried on in the name of Paul VI, whose letter *Octogesima Adveniens* is usually cited as a reference. It is as if Christians were invited in all good conscience to tread the path of socialism.

Insofar as the documents quoted are subject to free discussion among the people of God, it will readily be understood that a simple Catholic writer like myself does not hesitate from his place in society, in the line of his vocation, and on his own responsibility, to participate in this debate. This involves:

(1) the very substance of faith,
(2) the authority of the magisterium of the Catholic Church,
(3) the freedom of conscience,
(4) political freedom.

Does faith imply or even allow that the notion of "temporal liberation," an ambiguous one which has a socialist ring, be presented as it is today as an integral part of the Gospel and the message of salvation? It is impossible not to pose oneself this question first and foremost. In the preceding pages we have attempted to assemble the elements of the answer. Here we shall summarize the conclusions reached.

The gospels do contain a social message. It is the message of a filial love for the Father, of fraternal love for one's brothers. But this is not simply a natural love. It is a supernatural love with which God loves Himself. It is the love with which He loves us. In this love He calls us to love one another through Him, with Him, in Him and for Him. The social message of the Gospel is therefore a consequence of the divine adoption. This is true for all time, until the end of the world.

Christ did not come to reform temporal society. If at one

59

point He spoke of Himself as Liberator, in quoting Isaiah (Luke 4:18, Isa. 61:1-2), it was analogously, in order to make it clear that the liberation from sin—liberation from spiritual slavery with a view to heaven—is more important, more desirable still, than the temporal liberation of an oppressed people. He came to reestablish the Kingdom of God in souls, and then to unite these souls in the Kingdom of God. What is meant here is an inner kingdom, of a social relationship, in Him.

Nevertheless, precisely in order to further His teaching and the extension of the kingdom, Jesus did found a visible society: the Church. She is a city which has called man throughout the course of history to accept eternal salvation and which, as such, has no need to be incarnated in foreign social structures. She is, herself, an institution constituted around her Head Who is sacramentally, and therefore visibly and humanly, too, present among us. It is within this supernatural society that the evangelical justice is restored to man through baptism and the other sacraments. It is within the heart of the Church that the true evangelical liberation takes place with a view to the second coming.

In the Church, Christ, in uniting us to Himself, calls us to love one another, as sons of the same Father, as children of the same family, as members of the same Body whose Head He is—in short, the people of the same God. We succeed in doing this to the extent to which He becomes our life, and to which each of us can say with Paul of Tarsus, "I live, yet not I, but Christ lives in me."

Our relation to Him can, then, be that of the first Christians, because Jesus will be all in all, and as soon as He is all in all one can say of us, because it can be seen, "See how they love one another."

From all these points of view the message of the gospels is both personal and social, both mystical and visible. Within the Church it communicates supernatural love, both filial and fraternal. In no way does it lead to the welding on of a message of temporal liberation—both ambiguous and socialistic—to the social message of the gospels, or to making the former a necessary dimension of the latter. This is not so today, and will never be so.

A second question then arises. The living force of the Gospel cannot fail to exercise an influence in and through the Church, an action on human society which at times can be decisive. What are, from this point of view, the implications of the Gospel? Are they, now or ever, a temporal liberation, a concept ambiguous because of its inaccuracy and loaded with socialistic overtones?

Grace elevates nature, perfects it and repairs it. It does not change it. It does not transform it into another nature. It does not destroy it.

The gospels bring us God's revelation. They do not bring us the explicit knowledge of man and of human nature which man is capable of apprehending by his own powers. This is so, though the gospels do make more than one allusion to this knowledge. But even though in theory our reason can attain this true and certain knowledge of a natural law put in the soul by the Creator, in these matters the human spirit labors under the senses, the imagination, the appetites, disordered by the loss of original justice. As a result, Providence has led the Roman pontiffs to formulate this natural law, of which the Catholic Church has, from her very beginning, affirmed the existence.[7]

Especially since the reign of Leo XIII, throughout the first industrial revolution, followed by the second, the Church has expounded it with an ever-increasing precision with respect to economic-social situations. The popes have all equally affirmed that this natural law is the *foundation* of the social teaching of the Church. They have presented it in all its purity, precisely because they have been anxious to have it conform completely with the precepts of the Gospel, and have benefited from the charisma attached to this conformity, untarnished by error.

As its name indicates, this law, in its very essence, arises out of the moral necessities of nature and *not* from the contingencies of history. It is therefore not an ambiguous, socialistic or communistic, or Marxist or Freudian liberation which is implied in the announcement of eternal salvation, and which brings us an ex-

---

7 Cf. Romans 1:18-32.

trinsic testimony of its credibility. It is the natural law, which is in fact a constitutive dimension of the teaching of the Gospel.

It will be said that it is the spirit of Vatican II to present the message of salvation in the language of men of today, and that, consequently, it is more opportune to speak of man's liberation than to evoke natural law. I would not contest this if, in speaking of man's liberation, one truly drew the mind to the Gospel, and to its implications with respect to natural law. But this is not the case. On the contrary, the impressive number of examples of the binding of two incompatible concepts, which we have given, testify to the fact that the Gospel is being placed at the service of politics. Moreover, the attraction of salvation has become a bait or a pressure used to sway both Christians and other men, day after day, without, however, disclosing the final aim of this process toward a social revolution—a social revolution which is the very opposite of natural law, as *everyone knows only too well*. So then what? It is high time to recall the teaching of St. John: it is truth that frees (John 8:30, 47) and not equivocations. Still less, insinuations.

The real problem, the basic one, is man—human nature. Does it exist? What is it? Is what Marx, Nietzsche, Freud, Sartre or Reich have to say about it as compatible with the Gospel as what Aristotle said about it two thousand three hundred years ago, or Thomas Aquinas seven hundred years ago, or even John XXIII ten years ago? Can it be claimed that the Church has lost a hearing among men by her attachment in moral and social doctrine to the stale myth, both antiquated and ridiculous, of human nature? Some think so. Those who work toward imposing on us a Gospel welded to the socialist ideology through action on a huge scale, in a progressive mode, have let themselves be persuaded by atheistic thinkers that we must continue to adhere to the Gospel, but not to natural law or to human nature. The document, *Justice in Paris*, states the problem as follows: "Morality can no longer present itself as a body of norms conditioning both personal and social life in a given society. In a universe in a *constant state of mutation* it can only be a morality of meaning, i.e., a morality which enables us to determine the *deep meaning of human acts*, and to indicate the ultimate spring behind the activity of both individuals and groups of men." While evoking "the norms inscribed in our nature," this text affirms that "it is at the very heart of existence and action that we must discover both the norms of judgment and the guidelines of action, thanks to the objective analysis of the situation peculiar to each man and to each people."[8]

If we rightly understand what this implies, it means that we shall no longer find in human nature the ends and laws governing human action. While taking into account the norms inscribed in nature (but the question is how? and to what extent?) the basic orientation of morality will result from the analysis of the situation and the meanings that can be attached to human behavior.

Incidentally, Marx believes that man has no essence in the natural and immediate sense of the term. His essence is a universal which is non-natural and mediated. It is the result of social ties and is the fruit of a concrete mediation brought about by social work.[9]

If it is granted that the world—and man—are in a perpetual state of change, then one can attempt to reconcile a liberation of a socialist style with the Gospel. In such a case, the person would no longer necessarily be the foundation, the subject, and the aim of social life.

Christians are told that the notions of substance, of nature, and of person are incomprehensible to the man of today. We are asked to enter into a universe of relationships and of projects. The unborn child in his mother's womb is approached exclusively as a "call to be born." The sense for the real is blurred through language.

But can one still speak of an authentically evangelical language? In order to answer this question, we must examine the approach that Christ Himself used to reveal Himself as Man and as God.

First of all, He identified Himself as the Son of Man.

Echoing Daniel's prophecy, Jesus presents Himself as the Son of Man. He affirms by the same token that the divine Messiah has

---

[8] *Presence and Dialogue of Paris.* Italics mine.
[9] Karl Marx, *Thesis on Feuerbach*, 1845, thesis IV, trans. by Rubel in "Chosen Pages for a Socialist Ethics."

been *born* of man, that He has (it is the same word) a human *nature*. Therefore there is a human race, a human species, a nature that exists in God's eyes.

Let us take note of the fact that Jesus does not call Himself "a son of man," but "the Son of Man." He expresses in the most concrete way possible not only what we express abstractly in saying that He had a human nature, but also that He is the perfect model, the ultimate expression and the exemplary cause of the same. Consequently, all mutations will always have to be judged in the light of Christ's humanity, the perfect human nature, the exemplary manhood, the alpha and omega of humanity.

It is only after those who follow Him are convinced of His humanity that Jesus will begin to hint at the fact, and then to answer openly the questions, acknowledging that He is the Son of God. Had He begun with this His disciples would have been led to believe that He had only a human appearance. It was therefore imperative that the reality of His humanity should be recognized first through reason (*recta ratio*), and then that this same reason, illumined by faith, should acknowledge the reality of His divinity.

Once again, Jesus does not refer to Himself as one son of God among others, but as *the* Son of God. He is not a son of God as those He will teach to say, "Father." Neither is He a prophet among other prophets. He is greater. He is begotten of the Father. He receives life from the Father. In abstract terms, He *is* of divine nature.

The apostles began to understand, then, that it was the same Word which was the Son of God, Eternal Word, and Son of Man, Incarnate Word. It is this unique Word which the Church has identified in defining it as a unique Person. The duality of natures cannot be understood without the unity of the Person.

If Jesus is both Son of God and Son of Man, the Gospel implies by the same token that God exists *and that man exists*, over and above any cultural determination or any social change.

But if man exists as nature, if man exists as person, the whole Marxist analysis becomes incompatible with the Gospel—in a more radical way yet, any ideological, socialistic or communistic idea is incompatible with the Gospel. If Jesus is true Man, then there is no other spiritual liberation than the one coming through the Word of

64

God and the sacraments of the Church. There is no temporal liberation other than respect, in all the dimensions of human nature and its law, for the natural law which has been purified and clarified throughout the two thousand years of activity of the Holy Spirit within the Church. There are no other norms of political liberation than this part of natural law which formulates objectively the demands of justice in the whole spectrum of social relationships and which the Church herself has taught us to call, like the ancients, *jus naturale*, natural law. It imposes itself first and foremost on human action. It cannot possibly lead to its mutilation.

Every equivocation concerning the liberation of man rests on an uncertainty, nay, even a negation concerning human nature, natural law, natural right. But it is this natural law, this natural right, which Jesus, true Man, has come to take up and restore. This has been the invariable teaching of the Church.

We even have tangible proofs of this. Before Christ, the deepest and wisest of men had attained only a very imperfect vision of natural law. It is because Christ has saved man with His nature and all its laws that John XXIII was able to make of it an outstanding and imperishable declaration in the most famous of his encyclicals, *Pacem in Terris*.

2. The Authority of the Magisterium

We sometimes hear and read, "John XXIII, yes . . . but Paul VI?"

A Catholic can give only one answer: Show me where Paul VI has denied a *single* one of the human rights uninterruptedly formulated by his predecessors! Show me where Paul VI has ever denied the existence of human nature. Show me where Paul VI has ever denied the existence of the *human person*. Against these charges, we can indicate where Paul VI has affirmed the nature, the person and the rights of man.

First of all, let us refer to this passage of the *Credo* of June 30, 1968, which leaves no room for any ambiguity, any equivocation, any insinuation:

We believe in Our Lord Jesus Christ, Who is the Son of

65

God. He is the Eternal Word, born of the Father before time began, and one in substance with the Father, *homoousios to Patri*, and through Him all things were made. He was incarnate of the Virgin Mary by the power of the Holy Spirit, and was made man: equal therefore to the Father according to His divinity, and inferior to the Father according to His humanity, and Himself one, not by some impossible confusion of His natures, but by the unity of His person.

It should be clear from this brief passage, and in complete harmony with the Gospel that the Pope affirms here:

(1) that Christ is a *person*;
(2) that He is *consubstantial* with the Father;
(3) that He is the *Son* of God;
(4) that He is the Son of Man;
(5) that there is no confusion of the two natures.

Concerning human rights, in the letter *Octogesima adveniens,* Paul VI does not enumerate them exhaustively as John XXIII did in *Pacem in Terris.* He does not elaborate further the question of the right to property. There is no need to do so. But he refers to the complete enumeration of rights (see no. 16). Moreover, he sheds light on this document, which is clearly pastoral rather than doctrinal, by the request addressed to Christians and formulated as early as no. 4, *to draw the principles of their thinking, the norms of their judgment and the directives for their action* in the encyclicals and the acts of the ordinary magisterium in social matters, which together constitutes the authentic social doctrine of the Church. *"Ut principia cogitandi, judicandi normas, regulas operandi et sociali doctrina Ecclesiae hauriant."*[10] One cannot be clearer. It is the social doctrine of the Church which is in question. Who would dare insinuate that these words are to be understood in a sense other than the obvious?

Do they want to convince us that these texts should be distorted in order to make them concur with a socialist ideology which Paul VI, following his predecessors, has also condemned? Are they trying to bring us, in practice, to overlook the constant and solemn affirmations regarding the respect of legitimate politi-

---

[10] *Octogesima Adveniens,* no. 4, Latin text O.R., May 15, 1971.

cal authority as well as the right of property, even the goods of production?

An ever-increasing number of texts tend in this direction. The insidious linking of incompatible ideas ushered in by the uncertainties created by language welds together the ambiguous liberation of a socialist stamp with the redemption of Jesus on the cross. It clearly scorns Catholic doctrine. From this point of view, it is an open challenge, a disobedience which is spreading and has become a scandal with respect to the consistent teaching of both the Church and the reigning Pope.

We say this because the very authority of the magisterium is at stake. What will happen to the Church if, through a planned campaign, the conviction were to spread that in social matters the teaching of Pope Paul VI is opposed to the teaching of John XXIII, Pius XII, Pius XI, Benedict XV, St. Pius X, Leo XIII and Pius IX, to limit the list to the latest pontiffs? The speculation is particularly disturbing when one takes into account that according to the teaching of Pius XII, "The right of both the individual and the family to private property *immediately derives from the nature of the person.*"[11] It is the very concept of redemption which is thereby upset when it becomes doubtful that the person has been liberated through Jesus Christ, with regard to a fundamental part of his activity, namely the management of property.

In my humble opinion, the teaching of Paul VI must be defended against those who, either in theory or in practice, set him in opposition to his predecessors, and try to rally the faithful in favor of a socialist liberation, as they seem to have done in 1968 for the liberation of priests.

3. Liberty of Conscience

This is to be feared. If the present trend gains impetus, if the pairing of incompatible ideas continues and extends itself, it should become evident that within a few months public opinion will deny the right to any person, *not an acknowledged socialist, to call himself a Catholic.* This turns the teaching of Pius XI upside

---

[11] Pius XII, message dated September 14, 1952.

down. Unfortunately it is not hard to imagine a situation in which the socialists, having taken hold of the government, would grant the Church religious liberty only insofar as she would endorse the ideological slavery of social collectivism. The Church would then be expected to deny the teaching of John XXIII where he reminds us that "the right to private property, even of means of production, is valid *for all times*, for it is part and parcel of the natural law according to which man is prior to society, which must be ordered toward him as its end."[12] This right is valid *for all times*, for today and tomorrow.

The agents of this identification of redemption with temporal liberation, and salvation in Christ with the abolition of the right to private property, come to the point of exacting from the Christian, *in the name of the Gospel, that he acknowledge society to be prior to the person.*

One will therefore be urged, in the name of eternal salvation, to mutilate nature. In the name of justice in the world, the worst possible injustice toward man will be propagated, stripping him of his personal dignity. "An idea of false redemption,"[13] to use the word of Pius XI, will have been amalgamated with the true and unique redemption of Jesus Christ. The light and power of redemption will have been enslaved and falsified in order to use it as an instrument of the false ideology of collectivism.

Can we even imagine the refined and atrocious moral torture of a Church where the socialist liberation would become an integral part of the Gospel? The texts quoted above should be re-read carefully. Where do they bring us except to this violation of conscience?

4. Political Liberty

In welding redemption to temporal liberation, salvation in Christ to liberation "from any and every oppressive situation" with the idea of abolition of private property of the goods of

---

[12] *Mater et Magistra*, no. 109.
[13] Encyclical, *Divini Redemptoris*, no. 8.

production, the evangelical message is used, possibly with good intentions, in order to instate the most inhuman and the most irreversible political slavery ever established on this planet. We shall return to this point later, in examining the anatomy of totalitarianism.

The conclusion is unquestionable. The welding of Christ's Gospel to the call to socialist revolution is incompatible with the Christian faith.

4

Is Property a Sin?

The essential problem of our times
Is property unjust in itself?
The necessary involvement

From the point of view of the proclamation of the Gospel, is it possible to consider the right to property as an objective obstacle to the announcement of salvation?

Do the gospels contain a social message? Yes. It is the invitation to live as adopted sons of God, in theological charity, practicing the second commandment. Does this commandment to love one another in Christ imply a struggle for liberation? Yes, if we mean by that an interior fight against sin, which reforms our will in order to make it conform more and more to the demands of justice and charity. Yes, indeed, according to the consistent teaching of the Church, if it means putting her social doctrine into practice, in which natural law and revelation converge. But certainly not, if what is aimed at is abolition of absolutely fundamental natural rights, under the cover of liberation—and this is the intention of contemporary advocates of the total liberation of man.

Under these conditions the fusion which is being imposed all over, between the Gospel and liberation from any oppressive situation is inacceptable from the point of view of faith. This fusion constitutes a revolt against the constant teaching of the Church, including that of Paul VI. It results in turning the teaching of the Gospel, and of all the organizations which claim to be linked to the Church, into instruments at the service of a leftist political ideology. Through ambiguities and insinuations this fusion disfigures faith and tortures consciences.

Such are the conclusions we have now reached.

At this point in our reflections, the temporal liberation identified with the Gospel is seen as the result of a kind of reasoning promoted everywhere by propaganda, and which can be summarized as follows:

(1) The key problem of our times, seen in the light of the Gospel, is injustice in the world.

(2) Injustice results from any dependence on a man or group of men who control means of production as private property.

(3) Consequently, the first and most urgent step demanded by faith is to involve oneself in helping men of our time establish a collectivistic government.

Each of these three propositions deserves and demands a critical examination.

The Key Problem of Our Times

The synodal document on justice in the world claims that "a multitude of injustices constitutes the very core of the problems of our times." The Spanish document, *Justice and Peace* follows the very same line: "The question of justice is today the most serious and the most important for the whole of humanity. This is also true for us." The document, *Justice and Development in the Region of Paris,* is not less eloquent: "On the level of faith, development appears as a story which must turn out well, through all and for all." As for the Catholic Committee Against Hunger, during Lent 1972 it distributed a poster among the parishes of France, the text of which pushes this thesis to its last consequences: "Is it possible to be happy as long as a single man dies of injustice and hunger?" There is no need to multiply examples; they are abundant.

Moreover, the very structure of this kind of propaganda is not limited to putting the general problem of the temporal liberation of justice in the first place in order of urgency. The prevailing tendency is to establish a series of word equivalents which reduce all Christian notions to one: equity in the distribution of goods is the central aim of the Church in the world today. Faith, it is added, is nothing but justice. Love, we are told, is above all an absolute demand of justice. The Church's apostolate, it is added, will enjoy credibility to the extent that it is imbedded in the movement of an action for the sake of justice.

In short, under the pretext of interpreting the signs of the times, and to have a religion adapted to the men of today in an explicit fashion and with an uproar which I do not dare call infernal, one is led to the identification of religious faith with temporal justice, to claim that the first task of faith is to fight for justice. The striving for temporal justice is, in its turn, considered to be a precondition for any apostolate. This is even pushed to such a point that we are led to expect, on this earth, the fulfillment of a development of justice which has succeeded *through* all men and *for* all men, even of a world peopled by three and a half billion men, *none* of whom is ever to die of injustice!

From the simple viewpoint of common sense, it should be clear that we are dealing with plain demagoguery of the worst possible kind—religious demagoguery. To make us hope that the commitment of the Church in political matters will finally bring about the realization *on this earth,* now, or perhaps in the near future, of a world where injustice will be abolished, every tear dried, etc., can foster, in very upright souls, expectations which are as mad as they are vain. Their deception, sooner or later, is bound to be terrible. They will inevitably turn *against faith* which, having been identified with a terrestrial hope, will strike them as an abominable lie. Any effort to make them realize that they have misunderstood will be vain. *They will have texts to prove that they have been cheated.*

Even if this particular aspect is not the deepest one, it is fitting that we insist on it. Those who make the credibility of faith rest on the promises of temporal justice do not seem to be aware that this attitude leads, not to a religious faith, but simply and purely to using the Church to bring about a paradise of social justice on this earth.

And then there is faith.

The justice Jesus brought to this earth is the reconciliation of man with God. The reconciliation between man and man can only be a consequence of the former.

Jesus gave us a new life, the life of sons of God to those who believe His Word and enter into the Church. It is this new life which, while making us sons of the Father, renders us capable of being brothers in Christ.

Grave as temporal injustices may be—they were also numerous at the time of Herod—the essential question for the Christian is first and foremost to seek the Kingdom of God and His justice. It is not, it cannot be, to seek first and foremost the kingdom of man and his justice.

Christ has come so that His grace may enable man to mortify his passions, crucify his lust. When rooted in Christ, man accepts this way of life. He becomes able—but this is a consequence—to act in a more human and more Christian fashion, i.e., in greater harmony with both justice and charity.

To present the Gospel as a direct demand for exterior social justice, and make this a condition for the authenticity and credibility of interior and spiritual justice, is to invert it radically. The opposite is true. The Gospel presents a direct and immediate demand for spiritual, interior justice: filial toward the Father, fraternal toward our brothers. Exterior justice must be a consequence of interior justice, not vice versa.

Jesus multiplied the loaves with a view to the Eucharist. He did not institute the Eucharist with a view to multiplying loaves.

Jesus changed water into wine with a view to the sacrifice of Calvary. He did not accept the sacrifice of Calvary with a view to the miracle of Cana.

The Gospel is thus turned inside out, literally, as a garment is turned inside out. Everything may be there, but everything is distorted.

Thus, the first proposition of the campaign for temporal liberation waged in the name of the Gospel is untenable. It is contrary to faith. Today, as well as in the past, the second commandment is a consequence of the first. The reconciliation between man and man is a result of the reconciliation that has taken place between man and God—not the other way around. The slightest equivocation on this point is to be rejected.

We must not let ourselves be convinced that in claiming that God should be served first, we are detracting from the service which should be rendered to man. The whole history of the Church proves the opposite to be true—and in particular the history of Catholic social action.

Since 1891 the latter has played a particularly important and even decisive role in the social progress achieved in Western countries. It has contributed to curtailing the demands of the liberal mentality, while refusing to fall into the tyranny of the socialist mentality. Assuming freedom without a moral liberalism, and assuming at the same time the will to justice without totalitarian collectivism, it has helped (in spite of the spread of unbelief and immorality) to save the basic elements of a familial politics, a right to work, at times carefully elaborated, the dialogue and collaboration between the classes with a view to achieving social progress, the fruits of which are today clearly apparent. To deny all this, or rather to ignore or despise it, manifests a tragic blindness to facts.

That these results do not suffice cannot be denied. I am convinced that our efforts should be doubled to follow the guidelines of the social doctrine of the Church. But the central question, the *unum necessarium,* remains the Kingdom of God and His justice. Society will only become more fraternal, and therefore more equitable, to the extent that there are ardent Christians in every social stratum. The first Christians held all their possessions in common because they loved one another, through grace, as children of the same Father. It was not because they held everything in common that they eliminated "the objective obstacles" to a teaching and a holiness that were to come afterwards. There is a substantial error here, an evident error, an error which a Christian cannot allow to arise without quietly affirming the truth.

Is Ownership in itself Unjust?

If this first proposition (identifying the Gospel with economic considerations rather than with spiritual and supernatural presuppositions) is propagated widely and without precaution, the second proposition, on the contrary, remains on the level of an insinuation, and somehow seems to be presented with a certain shame. It suggests that injustice in this world results from a bond of dependence, and therefore from the inequalities which the practice of private ownership of the means of production brings about. It insinuates that, confronted with this situation, class struggle and alliance with revolutionary parties and syndicates is acceptable from a Christian standpoint.

The documents are padded. The mentality which "beatifies possession" is condemned by one. Another asks gravely whether liberation will be brought about "by the transformation of hearts or by the struggle between the classes." The third describes the situation of the contemporary world "as marked by the grave sin of injustice," as if contempt of God, debauchery, theft, murder, adultery, fraud, jealousy, envy, slander, pride, and personal acts of injustice were not also grave sins, and were less widespread! The document, *Justice and Development in the Region of Paris,* does not conceal a dialectic analysis of society. Endorsing the Marxist myth, it conceptualizes "the opposition, either conscious or unconscious, of property owners to the development of the deprived," and teaches that social revolution is a law of society founded on private ownership. "A person, a people, who aims at self-development nurtures a project which he intends to realize, and this project usually re-questions the social, economic, political equilibrium in which the affluent are settled. The dominated challenge the power of the dominators." All this is (of course) veiled; the "project" is not specified, the revolution is a mere "reexamination of the power of domination" in order to get rid of the affluent. The leading idea is unmistakable, even though its formulation may be muddled.

Nevertheless, it is worth asking ourselves why the campaign for temporal liberation in the name of the Gospel should be both so general and so padded, so insistent and yet so evasive, regarding the reexamination of the right to private property. It is because for practically all of this propaganda it is possible to take words or phrases of the Gospel and alter their meaning through misuse. The word liberation can be used—it is there in the Gospel; and it can be given a meaning related to temporal injustices rather than to Satan. The kinship between the meanings is a real one. Equivocation is easy.

Concerning private ownership, including that of means of production, the uneasiness of these propagandists cannot be overlooked. Apart from some Christians, socialists from youth onward, and from certain *avant-garde* religious personalities, the authors of these texts generally limit themselves to a few allusions. In order to avoid getting to the heart of the matter, they only specify that the Church offers no concrete solution of a social, political or economic nature to the question of justice in the world. It is claimed at the same time that "the very mission Christ confided to His Church is not of an economic or social order," a fact which is evident, manifest and fundamental, and at the same time that "the mission to preach the Gospel today requires a total commitment for the total liberation of man . . ." Radical—total—even though this *engagement* is not the key mission of the Church. The arguments begin to approach incoherence.

This incoherence is symptomatic. This opposition to private ownership which is both tenacious and inconsistent betrays an obvious uneasiness. This is the most difficult step to take in the ideological campaign which tries to identify openness to the world with openness to leftist political ideologies. Why? Because, quite providentially all popes have been so precise, solemn and unified in their affirmation of the right to property and denunciation of the class struggle that it is not easy to twist their words and alter their meaning.

Thus Pius XI, in order to establish that the right of private ownership was a constant and accepted doctrine of the Church, insisted upon the fact that popes and theologians "have unanimously held that it is from *nature* and therefore from the *Creator* that men have received the right to private ownership."[1]

And again, Pius XII taught that "the Christian conscience cannot acknowledge the justice of a social order which denies in

---

[1] *Quadragesimo Anno,* no. 50.

principle, or which renders impossible or vain the natural right to ownership of goods for private use as well as means of production."[2]

Just ten years ago, John XXIII reaffirmed that the value of this right is permanent—that is to say, that it remains valid independently of historical or cultural contingencies. "The right of private ownership *(jus privati dominii)* even over the means of production has a permanent value, for the very reason that it is a natural right, founded upon the ontological and teleological priority of individuals over society."[3]

This teaching of the immediate predecessors of Paul VI is, incidentally, the continuation of a teaching which is implicit in the gospels.

These, which so outspokenly condemn the spirit of wealth, do not at all identify the rich with the owner of an enterprise. The parable of the workers of the last hour would certainly not have been told by Jesus in the way it was, if He had judged that the system of private ownership and wage-earning was to be condemned *as such.* For the owner of vineyards referred to in the parable is the head of an enterprise. He owns a farm, and goes out early in the morning "to hire workers for his vineyard." He negotiates a salary contract:

> He made an agreement with the workers for one denarius a
> day, and sent them to his vineyard.

To those hired in the course of the day he also gives one denarius, that is to say, a wage calculated not on time expenditure or output but on the necessities of life.[4]

It is clear that this teaching is supposed to make us understand that in the heavenly kingdom, those who come last could very well be given first place. But it is equally clear that the examples chosen by Jesus in the order of economic life cannot be immoral ones in themselves.

---

[2] September 1, 1944.

[3] *Mater et Magistra,* no. 109.

[4] Matthew 20:1-16. Incidentally, this is also the teaching of Pius XI on right wages. *(Quadragesimo Anno,* no. 108-109 and 70-82.)

Therefore, according to the Gospel, the possession of a means of production is in conformity with nature. Again, according to the Gospel, the making of a contract between a worker and an owner of capital is also in conformity with nature. From both a purely human and a Christian point of view, therefore, it is possible that an employer be not only just, but also good. ("Why be envious because I am generous?") Man has been weakened by original sin, not corrupted.

There is, therefore, no law of inevitable opposition among the various social classes. There is no law of opposition between those dominating and those dominated. Never did Jesus, even in the remotest sense, preach the revolt of slaves. He brought about the conversion of their masters and this proved to be much more efficacious. The teaching of St. Paul at the end of the first epistle to Timothy is clear. He advises the rich not to put their hopes in uncertain wealth, and to give with generosity and liberality. He teaches the slaves neither revolt nor belligerence.

> All slaves "under the yoke" must have unqualified respect for their masters, so that the name of God and our teaching are not brought into disrepute. Slaves whose masters are believers are not to think any the less of them because they are brothers; on the contrary, they should serve them all the better, since those who have the benefit of their services are believers and dear to God.[5]

This doctrine is also to be found in the Church fathers. Vehement against wealth, they do not question the exercise of the right to property, but rather the way in which it is used when it produces monopoly.

It is likewise the doctrine of St. Thomas Aquinas, the *doctor communis*.[6] It is taught throughout *Rerum novarum* by Leo XIII. Paul VI solemnly celebrated the eightieth anniversary of this encyclical—not in order to contradict its essential content, as has sometimes been suggested, but rather in order to confirm it, as we have already stated above.

---

[5] I Timothy 6:1-2.

[6] *Summa Contra Gentiles* III, 127 and II, III, q. 66, a. 2.

This is why Christian collectivists are, on this fundamental issue, both insistent and inconsistent. They try to spread a certain state of mind among Catholics. But at the same time they proclaim that the Church has no social doctrine in order that, following the logic of the state of mind they have themselves spread, Catholics feel in conscience compelled to vote for atheistic and collectivistic parties, and eventually to participate in a violent social revolution. The apostolic intention of this plan does not prevent it from being the worst possible chimera.

Christian collectivists have no valid evangelical basis for their conduct. They cannot invoke any teaching of the Church favorable to their cause. Both scripture and tradition agree in the teaching of a completely different doctrine.

Jesus did not come to tear man away from His natural rights. He came to give man back the supernatural light and strength to make good use of these rights. He came, even, to teach men, in certain cases where it was a special vocation, to renounce this use.

Concerning the right to marriage, the Catholic doctrine is well known. It teaches that marriage is a sacrament; that is to say, that the consent of the two baptized partners is efficacious, in obedience to the Church, in communicating to them all the graces necessary to live according to their state: a single man and a single woman indissolubly united until the death of one of them, reciprocally faithful to a love that expresses itself in the conception and education of their children.

So we see that Jesus does not slacken natural law. He reinstates monogamy. He can do this because His grace brings to the spouses who collaborate with it the possibility of remaining faithful throughout all difficulties.

He goes further. He requests of some that they become "eunuchs for the Kingdom of God." He sanctifies marriage and, simultaneously, He offers to those whom He has called in a special way, the renunciation of the use of the right to marriage, in taking a vow of chastity.

The same doctrine is applicable by extension to the right of ownership. It is taught that the management of goods can and must conform to justice. The Christian must even, in the spirit of the beatitudes, "possess as if possessing nothing," that is to say, administer the goods confided to him with the detachment of poverty. Of some, finally, Jesus requests the vow of poverty, i.e., the renunciation of the exercise of the right of ownership. But even the necessity of renunciation proves, by contrast, that the right of ownership exists, and that it is inscribed in human nature.

As may be surmised from the preceding, Christian collectivism is bound to be a contradiction in terms. For, because of His respect for the freedom of souls, our Lord did not give equal weight to the evangelical precepts and the counsels which have been added to them. Regarding material goods, the precepts themselves demand that Christians avoid any sin against justice. This objective norm is very exacting in the economic sphere, concerning prices or wages, or the use of capital or the contribution to justice in general. The evangelical counsels, in turn, go much further: "If you wish to be perfect, go and sell what you own and give the money to the poor. . . ."[7] These counsels, however, are addressed neither to all men nor to all times. In contradistinction to the precepts, failure to live up to them does not entail any sin, except for those who have freely taken on the obligation to practice them.

This is why the claim that the Gospel implies somehow the communal possession of goods, and consequently the abolition of private ownership, spiritually amounts to making of the evangelical counsel of poverty a strict and universal precept, and it is precisely this which our Lord did not do.

Moreoever, *today as well,* it is completely possible to control means of production, even if they are considerable, and still to act according to the spirit of poverty. The campaign of slanders directed against certain heads of enterprises, especially on the part of certain ecclesiastical circles, constitutes not the least noticeable form of injustice in this world. Having been professor for more than fifteen years at the School of Business Executives of Christian Patronage, I have dealt with several thousand business executives. I have corrected their papers on social doctrine. I can only wish

---

[7] Matthew 19:21.

that many antagonistic priests had some of their balance and generosity.

Possession is no sin. The private owner of means of production, whether an individual or a society, is not a public sinner. The evangelical precept implies the practice of the virtue of justice and constitutes a strict moral obligation. The evangelical counsel which implies renunciation of all forms of ownership cannot be transformed into a social structure without turning into a torture for consciences.

If in times past people could be scandalized by the cases (in fact very rare) of parents who forced their daughters into the convent, to follow the evangelical counsels by force, what must be said of the revolutionaries who, abolishing in fact the natural right of private ownership, want to corner an entire population through a magical spiritual mutation, though everyone knows that this kind of change actually requires a special vocation, a slow maturation and a totally free sacrifice.

Finally, there is obedience! Man has a natural right to be the responsible cause of his actions. Nature is such that, according to a particular point of view, human relationships are hierarchical, i.e., based on the right of the superior to create moral obligations in conformity with right reason—obligations which the inferior is called upon to fulfill. It is only certain souls who are asked by Christ to renounce the exercise of the universal right to be the responsible cause of one's own actions by taking a vow of obedience.

However, in a collectivist society, the necessity of authority and obedience is not abolished. Rather it imposes on each person total renunciation of the right to be the responsible cause of one's own acts. Indeed, when the right to private property is respected, one can change one's foreman or manager, and this takes place every day in free countries. *One cannot change society when it is the society which owns everything and makes all decisions.* A vow of obedience is imposed which is obligatory, universal and irreversible.

Collectivism is therefore a caricature of the Gospel. It is community of goods without grace. It is evangelical poverty without vocation. It is detachment from ownership without freedom. It is renunciation of the right to be responsible for one's acts, without grace, without vow, without vocation, superimposed upon all. It is absolute tyranny. The Christians who want to establish this hell on earth in the name of the Gospel should rather give incredible counter-testimony to it.

Possession, including private possession of the means of production, is in itself not unjust. The owner is not a public sinner. It is urgent that people's mentality be corrected on this point— and people's hearts as well.

The Necessary Involvement

Then you object to changing anything? You think things are going well? You even fail to share the judgment of the Pope, himself, who asks of us a commitment for a more just world?

Thus the Christian collectivists proceed dialectically. They endorse the Marxist scheme: either oppressive capitalism or liberating socialism. And they argue: if you are not for the second, you are necessarily an accomplice of the first, at least unconsciously. From then on your trial begins—in the name of the Gospel, of course.

All we can do is to challenge the tyranny of this scheme in the name of the very teaching of the Council and of Paul VI, who has proclaimed that, "The same Christian faith can lead to different commitments."[8] The Church does, indeed, have a social doctrine. It affirms *both* the legitimacy of the right of ownership, even of the means of production, and at the same time the co-management, not of private enterprise, which belongs to owners, but of professions and of the whole economic organism. It calls for a *prise de conscience* of common interests, of negotiations and agreements on improvements, through constant modification of the equity of relations and working conditions as well as the assessment of goods and services.

This is the natural order. It tends to reconcile private ownership with the national community of all participants in the produc-

---

[8] *Gaudium et Spes,* no. 43; *Octogesima Adveniens,* no. 50.

83

tive effort. It leads to the reconciliation of classes by demanding of them a progressive disarmament and to the replacement of the opposition of forces by adjustment of rights. It also implies demanding that owners of capital as well as from heads of syndicates become increasingly conscious of their mutual responsibilities and the concrete problems they are called upon to solve. It should be the concern of the state to facilitate sound relationships in the working world.

It follows from the very logic of friendship and of the spirit of collaboration that the results of these dialogues, this organic collaboration should lead to a better reciprocal understanding, a quicker detection of tacit injustices, and should facilitate an immediate abolition of them. But to imagine that man will cease to be domineering, envious, jealous, covetous, dishonest, etc., if in practice the right of ownership were abolished, is an incredible flight of fancy. We only need witness the passions which develop within communistic regimes, the oft-recurring purges, and the dramatic situations which arise among workers in Poland, Chile, Yugoslavia, China and the USSR.

It is truly incredible to see how men allow themselves to be misled by errors refuted 2,300 years ago:

> One hears it said that the evils actually existing in the states are attributable to the fact that the goods are not possessed in common . . . In reality, these evils are never caused by the lack of the community of goods, but by human weakness.

And Aristotle continues, as if he himself had experienced our modern, popular democracies:

> For we ascertain that those who possess goods in common or all together have among themselves much more frequent conflicts than those citizens whose interests are separate.

He finally adds:

> Moreover, it would be just to indicate not only the evils of which men would be freed in adopting the community of goods, but also the advantages of which they would be deprived; then it is manifest that the way of life they would have to lead is absolutely intolerable.[9]

---

[9] Aristotle, *Politics,* Book II, chapter v.

The Iron Curtain, the Bamboo Curtain and the Wall of Shame are all eloquent testimonies of this statement and confirm the realism of the author of *Politics*. Hundreds of thousands of men and women have risked death, and many been assassinated in order to flee from the paradises of collective redemption.

It is not the abolition of a right inscribed in nature that liberates man. It is the redemption of Jesus Christ who heals through grace, step by step, the weakness of each of us, and gives us the strength to endure the weakness of others.

The social suppression of the right of ownership is incompatible with the created order. It contradicts the Gospel in transforming the counsel of poverty into a strict and universal precept. This is not redemption; it is mutilation.

Under these conditions, to claim that today the right of ownership constitutes an objective obstacle to the proclamation of the Gospel amounts to falsifying the nature of the most certain and best established teaching of the Gospel, affirmed by the Church herself.

5

Socialism with a Human Face

Objections
Definition of Socialism
Socialism and the Sciences

Is socialism with a "human face" realizable and compatible with the natural order inscribed in man?

From the preceding thoughts a conclusion becomes evident. I do not hesitate to formulate it here explicitly and uncompromisingly: *In my humble opinion socialism is today the most serious temptation Christians are confronted with, and the one most threatening to their faith.*

Some will object to this. I understand their annoyance, perhaps even their suffering or revolt. But they also worry me, because their reactions prove to what extent souls are infected with this kind of thinking.

I say "souls are infected" in the same sense that one might speak of a physical infection, for there are spiritual sicknesses. They are infectious just like the others are infectious, and are caught, more often than not, without knowing it, simply by breathing the "air of the time."

I also foresee objections! To tell the truth, they come from all sides.

—But they are not on the same plane; faith is related to the soul; socialism is a social and economic system.

87

—You have not truly understood the Council. Openness to the world means openness to socialism.

—The word puts you off, but you must learn to overcome this kind of intellectual inhibition. There is a positive message in socialism which you should discover. You just refuse to make the necessary effort!

—Your position sets up an obstacle to the Church's apostolate. The Church must penetrate into the working class. In proclaiming her opposition to socialism she bars the way to effective preaching of the Gospel in the world today.

—You fail to discern the signs of the times. Socialism is an inevitable revolution. There are several brands of it. Let us not mix everything up. If Christians fail to define their socialism as a socialism with a human face, they will be cut off from a world that will be made without them.

—In rejecting socialism, you make yourself the accomplice of capitalism, of the domination of monopolies, of the frenzied selfishness of the rich, and you compromise the Church in identifying her with the established disorder and entrenched plutocracy of our time.

—You are taking a grave risk! For if, tomorrow, the Church demanded that we become socialists, what would become of you? Would you consider cutting yourself off from the Pope and the bishops united to him? You'd better think twice!

Such are the objections which, even though not an exhaustive list, summarize the arguments of those who campaign for the Church to grasp the "historical chance" given her to participate with all men of good will who strive to establish "socialism with a human face."

Objections

I must admit that I am not impervious to these objections. On the one hand, they do express a vision to which a number of men and women have given their hearts, and for which they have, at times, risked their lives. And again, several of the arguments I have mentioned appeal to undeniable Christian realities: the duty of the Christian concerning the apostolate, and also concerning political

88

and social commitments. We cannot discard these problems with a wave of the hand. Finally, and forgive me if I draw an example from personal experience, numerous private and public dialogues on that very topic with men such as Georges Montaron[1] or Roger Garaudy[2] have granted me the opportunity to reach persons over and above the ideas that separated us. By the same token, I was able positively to grasp whatever sincere impetus there is to be found among some of the contemporary socialist leaders in the domains of thought and politics.

On the other hand, I cannot overlook the fact that what was formulated by Pius XI in 1931 is not a purely contingent argument, valid only at a given time, and in relation to certain historical circumstances. He wrote, "If socialism, like all errors, contains a portion of truth, it is nonetheless true that it rests on a theory of society of its own, and which is irreconcilable with authentic Christianity."

This is not an argument based on authority, but rather a conclusion reached by intellectual insight. We shall return to this point. It is because this teaching is related to a problem of the soul, and not only to a secondary and peripheral one, that I believe it timely to confront it with opposing arguments. It is a fair debate. I wish it could be a starting point for reflection for all those seeking, groping for, or affirming a solution. "Religious socialism, Christian socialism," Pius XI continued, "are contradictions in terms: no one can, at the same time, be a good Catholic and a good socialist."

When one grasps both the meaning and motive of this affirmation with a true inner understanding, he will truly be led to see that socialism is today the most momentous temptation for Christians, and the one most threatening to their faith.

First Objection: Christian faith and socialism cannot be placed on the same level. Faith is a matter of the soul. Socialism is a social

---

[1] Cf. dialogue on *Socialism,* edited by Beauchesne.

[2] Cf. the Round Table of "France-Inter" published in *l'Homme Nouveau,* October 20, 1968 (1, Place St. - Sulpice, Paris, 6°).

and economic system. Therefore, they cannot be set in direct op-
position. Normally these two spheres should be viewed as comple-
mentary.

Unfortunately, this is not the case. For, in fact, the Christian faith and socialism do meet on the same level. Socialism is not restricted to a purely economic plane. It is a philosophy of happiness, and unfolds itself in the spiritual domain. Christian faith, to the very extent that it is ordered toward salvation, includes implications concerning natural law. In practice, both claim, on a certain level, to bring *redemption*. It is here that their mutual antagonism is manifest.

Socialism opposes established disorders, social injustices, and, in short, *the sins of this world*. It claims that its cause is rooted in private economic activity, in free enterprise, and the resulting exchange, in the dictatorship of monopolies which allegedly accompanies it. The social redemption which derives from socialism consists in changing the form of society in establishing a collective control of economy, and thereby guaranteeing both social justice and the participation of workers.

Christianity, in its turn, teaches us that Christ came *to take on and to expiate the sins of the world*. The cause of this sin lies in the inherent frailty of fallen man. Christianity condemns the faults which result from unbridled love of money, but also those resulting from uncontrollable sensuality, and insatiable thirst for domination. Then, Christ forgives "seventy times seven" times the man who commits these sins, and grants him light and strength to liberate himself from it. For Christ's redemption is not for the purpose of changing the form of society, but of renewing the hearts of men and, through them, the face of this earth.

Thus, at this point we are facing *two interpretations of sin*. One of them basically ascribes sin to structures which allow man the freedom to exploit workers. The other attributes it to the basic frailty of the human will. We face *two plans of redemption*. One of them comes about through the reform of economic structures, the other through the renewal of persons and societies regenerated in Christ. And we face *two hopes*. The one in the merits of a collectivistic system which should realize the material aims of life according to an ideal of justice, the other in the virtue of each individual man, enlightened and strengthened through grace, and living interiorly according to the demands of justice and charity in order to fulfill God's will, on earth as in heaven.

This is why Pius XI, weighing his words carefully, claimed that it is impossible to be at the same time a *true* socialist and a *good* Christian, for the true socialist gives logical priority to the social struggle, the combat against the structures of certain individual rights, and against all those attached to these structures. When he comes into power, he will politically impose his vision of the fall (in the "capitalistic sin") and of redemption, according to the socialist way. The good Christian, on the other hand, gives priority to the interior struggle, to the spiritual confrontation, and puts his hope in the apostolate which transforms the very soul of society. Workers are the apostles to workers, executives the apostles to executives. Social justice results from a collaboration of the classes in a reciprocal effort to reach fraternal peace.

In the long run, both Christianity and socialism aim, therefore, at completely redirecting the orientation of the soul. Because socialism represents an ideal, it tends to take possession of the soul, and to form it according to its own aims and methods. On the other hand, Christ, according to Saint Paul, must be *everything* in everyone. On this level, the conflict between the socialist ideology and Christ is one of confrontation between two different mystiques, at the very heart of the interior life. We have had the opportunity to follow this debate very closely. To say that it is tragic is no exaggeration.

Should this not yet be clearly understood, let us make it clear: this is a debate which involves salvation itself. The temptation to impose justice on earth is subtle and seductive. It engages simultaneously generosity, virtuous pride, wrath against the rich, and stoical renunciation. It can mislead great and noble souls.

Second Objection: You have not truly understood the Council. Openness to the world means openness to socialism. The most profound meaning of aggiornamento is the transition from a Church within Christendom to a missionary Church. In other words, from a feudal, bourgeoise and static Church to a Church which is egalitarian, proletarian and advancing.

To meet this objection, we must first agree on a preliminary criterion: where is the true Council to be found? Is it in the texts of the Council itself? Or in the authorized interpretation which the Pope gives of it on the occasion of his teaching of the ordinary *magisterium*? Is it to be found in the at times divergent interpretations of certain bishops' conferences? Is it in the "spirit of the Council" in the sense propounded by some interventions of Cardinal Suenens? Finally, is it in the claim that Vatican II is only a starting point which has generally opened the paths to research in any and every direction?

This very enumeration suffices to make us understand how weak the aforementioned objection is. Those who claim that openness to the world means openness to socialism, but in a clandestine fashion and based on the "spirit of the Council" or on "the direction of history" of their own interpretation, are totally stripped of authority, except that of their own desire, which they mistake for reality.

If one is to abide by the Council and the Pope, this identification of openness to the world and openness to socialism does not hold. The Council is very clear: "Through her mission and her nature, the Church is bound to no particular form of culture, nor to any particular political, economic or social system."[3] In this text, there is, therefore, neither an openness to socialism nor to any other system.

There is even indication of a certain reserve with respect to socialism. This same document states that the Church is "both the sign and the safeguard of the transcendent character of the human person."[4] It is, essentially, this transcendent character of man which is neglected by socialism, which limits itself to the economic organization of society in its plan for human redemption.

If we now turn to the pontifical teaching, we shall see that

---

[3] *Gaudium et Spes*, 42.4.

[4] *Ibid.*, 76.2.

John XXIII has clearly distinguished between socialization and socialism, and that he has specified that "the economic world results from the personal initiative of single persons, whether they act individually or associated in various manners in pursuit of common interests."[5] As for Paul VI, he has reminded us forcefully "that the right of private ownership constitutes for no one an absolute and unconditional right"; he has underlined the gravity of the duties attached to it, in order to shed light upon the fact that this right exists with a view to its prudent usage, and that by abolishing it, we would abolish with it the very possibility of practicing justice.[6]

We thus see that those who claim that the Council has turned the Church toward socialism, find as little support in the texts of Vatican II as in the authorized teaching of the Sovereign Pontiffs. They give these a free and daring interpretation, to say the least.

Third Objection: The word, socialism, can put off those who have always rejected it by a sort of intellectual reflex. But there is a positive content in this word. Many people have put their hope in it. This is a good enough reason to use it, provided its meaning is defined.

We are not stubbornly resistant, and at times we have adopted the use of words in which we found little inspiration or dropped others that were very much to our liking. But when this has been done, it has been for a serious reason, and precisely on this ground we avoid using the word socialism in a positive sense.

To be more precise, I have given up granting a positive meaning to almost all "isms." In fact, the suffix, "ism," indicates more often than not a totalitarian system which centers on a particular reality thus idealized. The concept nation refers to something good. Nationalism is to be rejected. Liberty has something good. Liberalism is a very harmful error. The same holds true of reason and rationalism, nature and naturalism, individual

---

[5] *Mater et Magistra,* second part.
[6] *Populorum Progressio,* no. 23.

93

and individualism, society and socialism, and so forth.

In all these cases, a part of reality is made to become the center of reality. But the center of reality, the Alpha and Omega of all things, is Christ. We, therefore, are entitled to speak of Christianity and of Catholicism, though still on the condition of adoring Jesus Christ, and not his doctrine! But socialism, liberalism, individualism, communism, etc., are ideologies, abstract intellectual idols, each of which has already exacted bloody sacrifices like all idols. There were many in the nineteenth century who wanted to ally the Gospel with economic liberalism. It would be foolish to commit a similar mistake with respect to socialism.

Furthermore, the present sociological atmosphere is pervaded by such powerful psychological pressure tending in the direction of a revolution opposed to the natural right, that the use of the word socialism in a well defined sense, and truly in conformity with the natural law, would immediately become a psychological weapon in the hands of those who ceaselessly work at the moulding of public opinion.

Fourth Objection: Your position constitutes an obstacle to the apostolate of the Church. The Church should penetrate into the working class. In asserting her opposition to socialism she closes in advance the ways to effective preaching of the Gospel.

We must admit that in spite of the good intentions that lie behind this objection, it does not strike us as very forcible. Indeed, how could the Church, at the same time, make herself the champion of economic liberalism in order not to impede her apostolate in the North American capitalistic world, the advocate of existentialism, from fear of alienating Sartre's disciples; and a defender of structuralism, in order not to cut herself off from the followers of Lévi-Strauss? Apostolate means becoming all things to all men, but certainly not espousing any and every world view.

This is all the more true as the thesis formulated above is proposed only with regard to socialism. In fact, there are not two types of men: the workers to whom we should preach Jesus Christ in becoming socialists, and the non-workers, who should be con-

94

verted *at the same time* to Christ and to socialism. The result of this kind of thinking is easily foreseeable. Unfortunately it has already led some in its train.

Fifth Objection: You prove yourself incapable of reading the signs of the times. Socialism is an inevitable revolution. There are several brands of it. Let us not confuse everything. If Christians fail to define their socialism, a socialism with a human face, they will once again be alienated from a world that will be made without them.

For a long time we have been trying to discern the signs from God, an expression which strikes me as better and more precise than "the signs of the times." Now, just as the crisis of 1929 rang the death knell of economic liberalism throughout the world, the outbreak of "the Spring of Prague" in 1968 has marked the knell of all socialisms "with a human face." The socialisms of Moscow and Peking have long been known to be concentration camps from which escape is most difficult.

There is no hope for the various brands of "human" socialism, because in its very essence, this moderate regime is nothing but a reaction within "conservative" collectivism toward a bit of freedom and respect of the human person. And this dynamism leads, by natural inclination, to a regime in which economy will be based on the personal initiative of individuals. Its face will then be truly human when the regime in question is social, indeed, but without being socialistic!

Furthermore, there is no hope for a socialism with a human face because socialism with an *inhuman* face—which actually dominates a third of this earth will not (as has been proved) accept a dynamism that runs contrary to its direction of history, a dynamism that would rapidly become contagious in all countries either occupied by or satellites of Moscow or Peking.

Finally, there is no hope for a socialism with a human face because the Marxist analysis becomes more and more anachronistic. The political collapse of socialists in France is not a mere chance happening; neither is their electoral defeat in England to be interpreted as coincidental. Workers are increasingly becoming petits bourgeois. They are willing to enter into strikes aiming at reform, but they are not tempted by the revolution. They know that the administrative and bureaucratic virus of socialist countries sterilizes production, and, on the whole, they prefer to cope with neo-capitalism.

Sixth Objection: In rejecting socialism, you make yourself objectively an accomplice of capitalism, of the domination of monopolies, of the frantic selfishness of the rich, and you compromise the Church in linking her to the established disorder and the existing plutocracy.

The teaching of Pius XI, Pius XII, John XXIII and now Paul VI has led me to the belief that neither individualistic neo-capitalism, nor the various brands of socialism, are in conformity with the designs of God.

The communists and the socialists want to impose their thesis that there are but two possible political systems: capitalism and socialism. This is inaccurate. For the last hundred years, and still more forcibly in the course of the last twenty-five years, a certain social teaching has arisen. Young as it may be, it has more chance than any other to impose itself on the rubble of liberal capitalism and the various brands of socialism which flounder today. This social teaching is neither a magical recipe nor a system of the same brand as liberalism and socialism. It is the realization, both realistic and concrete, of a spirit of justice and charity in the institutions favoring a dialogue, and a collaboration between classes; economic life is then assumed by professional organisms, and equal interprofessionals.

These are not utopias. They actually exist and are progressing. And the social spirit, stripped of socialism, has, to its credit, more accomplishments than the socialist ideology. The Code of Work and all the agreements signed between social partners in various free countries are tangible realities.

Seventh Objection: You are taking a grave risk. If today the

96

Church were to make it a duty for us to become socialists, what would become of you? Are you willing to cut yourself off from the Pope and the bishops? You'd better be on your guard.

I must confess that this hypothesis strikes me as so improbable that I consider it to be a sheer product of the imagination. We only need recall the solemn words of Pius XI who, in *Quadragesimo Anno,* declared that socialism, if it remains true to its nature, cannot be reconciled with the principles of the Catholic Church. I quote here the essential text:

> Many are the Catholics who, realizing clearly that Christian principles can never be either sacrificed or minimized, seem to be raising their eyes towards the Holy See, and earnestly beseeching Us to decide whether or not this form of socialism has retracted so far its false doctrines that it can now be accepted without the loss of any Christian principles, and be in a sense baptized. In Our fatherly solicitude We desire to satisfy these petitions, and Our pronouncement is as follows: Whether considered as a doctrine, or as an historical fact, or as a movement, socialism, if it really remains socialism, cannot be brought into harmony with the dogmas of the Catholic Church, even after it has yielded to truth and justice on the points We have mentioned; the reason being that it conceives human society in a way utterly alien to Christian truth.[7]

The socialism that truly remains socialism threatens faith. It offers a social redemption which consists *not* in putting its hope in redeemed man so that he may use his rights as he should, but in abolishing these rights because man uses them badly.

But Christ has liberated us, in faith, hope and charity.

Definition of Socialism

Finally, there is an objection which is not on the same level as the preceding ones. It tends to make socialism evasive, or difficult to define. There are so many brands of it. Socialism as such, in

---

[7] *Quadragesimo Anno,* 116-117.

contra-distinction to capitalism, *does not exist!*

Let us specify some varying viewpoints.

Some affirm, "There are various definitions of socialism. Pius XI may have condemned one of them, but he could not have condemned them all—particularly those which did not exist in his time!" Others say, "Socialism is a very general word, so general that it defies definition. It rather refers to a general orientation which favors generosity over selfishness, equity over injustice." Others again claim, "Atheistic socialism is an ideology. But it is quite possible to separate the technical aspect of socialism from this trend. All difficulties would collapse as soon as it were enlightened, and even oriented toward the Christian faith."

Others again go into detail and explain, "What is the common bond existing between a Stalinist socialism based on tyranny and a socialism like that in Sweden founded on a fiscal equalizing of revenues? What is there in common between a static socialism, marked by Marxist inspiration, and a societary socialism tending toward auto-management, such as is advocated among Christian militants?"

These contradictory observations raise a single and unique problem concerning the definition of socialism.

Classical Authors

It is legitimate, first of all, to recall some definitions of socialism given by men who enjoy the authority to do so.

Pierre Mendès-France—seeking, as he has both recently and in the past, the conditions proper to a modern socialism—assigns to it as its aim, "what finally constitutes the aim of collective life, i.e., the improvement of the living conditions of man through the ever-increasing production of merchandises and goods."[8] He describes, as a basic means to reach this aim, "an active planning," i.e., the determination through the state of objectives that must be reached, and which will have to be accepted as such by the whole of the group."[9] The former president of the

---

[8] *L'Express*, April 7, 1960, p. 12.
[9] *Ibid.*, p. 13.

Council specified further that "the value of a social system depends primarily upon the rhythm of growth which it is capable of giving the economy, and the use it makes of the surplus production obtained to realize a fair distribution of wealth."[10]

I once asked Georges Montaron, the director of *Témoignages Chrétiens*, which definition of socialism he would favor. He answered by quoting the following text of André Philip: "Socialism is the action of workers to establish, through the intermediation of their organizations, a collective direction of economic life, and a socialization of monopoly enterprises, in order to hasten technical progress, guarantee a fair allotment of products, and to enable workers to partake of the responsibilities and essential decisions of economic and social life. . . ."[11]

In the framework of a general study on this question, Bourgin and Rimbert write on their side: "We shall define socialism as a form of society whose fundamental bases are the following:

(1) Social ownership of the instruments of production.
(2) Democratic management of these instruments.
(3) Orientation of production toward the meeting of human needs."[12]

Larousse terms socialism "the system of those who want to transform society through the incorporation of the means of production within society, the return of goods to the collectivity, the distribution among all of the common work, and consumer goods."

Pierre Mendès-France, André Philip, Georges Montaron are incontestably representatives of contemporary socialism. The synthesis of Larousse cannot be accused of being slanted; the same can be said of the one of Bourgin and Rimbert.

The Essence of Socialism

Now, all of these definitions say the same thing. Under diverse formulations, with different emphases, they all claim, without any possible ambiguity:

---

10 *Ibid.,* p. 14.
11 *Socialism,* G. Montaron and M. Clement, p. 10.
12 Bourgin and Rimbert, *Socialism,* p. 13 (P.U.F.)

(a) That socialism exists as an abstract notion. It is completely common to all those who use the term. None of these authors tells us that he is defining a particular socialism, but simply socialism.

(b) That the *aim* of socialism consists in the improvement of economic life: the increase of production, and justice in distribution.

(c) That the *means* to realize socialism is always to be found in a collectivization, whether of the means of production, or of the means of allotment. In other words, it presupposes the priority of society over the person.

Whether collectivization takes place in the top strata of society or at the lower levels, whether it is practiced on the level of ownership of production goods or on the level of consumer goods, in no way alters this fundamental implication that society holds priority over the person.

In 1931, more than forty years ago, Pope Pius XI defined the essence of socialism *in exactly the same way.*

(a) Pius XI examined the transformation undergone by socialism. The latter is to be rejected to the extent *"that it truly remains socialism."* This makes it clear that he was referring to socialism *as such*—i.e. the common denominator of basic assumptions upon which it rests and not to just one form of socialism.

(b) How does Pius XI define socialism that "remains truly socialism"? He tells us that socialism, through "its conception of society," overlooking the fact that in society man must act freely and uprightly, "assumes that the human community has been formed exclusively with a view to well-being."

Now, what does Mendès-France tell us? He states that "the aim of collective life is the improvement of the living conditions of man through the ever increasing creation of merchandises or goods." What does André Philip say? He claims that what is at stake "is to hasten the technical progress and guarantee a fair distribution of products." And what does Larousse say? "The distribution of common work and of consumer goods among all." What does Bourgin say? "Orientation of production toward satisfaction of men's needs."

In all these cases (excepting the statement of Pius XI) social life is viewed as *having* to be organized with a view to man's well being.

(c) According to Pius XI, the "socialism that remains truly socialism" is defined by the fact that "economic activity . . . must, of necessity, be socially led. From this necessity it follows, according to them, that men are bound, with respect to production"—and, we might add, with regard to consumption—"to deliver themselves or to subject themselves to society."

The conclusion of *Quadragesimo Anno* keeps its full validity, for it touches the very essence of socialism:

> Society, therefore, as socialism conceives it, is on the one hand impossible and unthinkable without the use of obviously excessive compulsion; on the other it no less fosters a false liberty, since in such a scheme no place is found for true social authority, which is not based on temporal and material well-being, but descends from God alone, the Creator and last end of all things.[13]

Socialism and the Sciences

Here we must insist that indeed, socialism, as it has just been defined, has repercussions in all domains.

From a theological point of view, it presents itself as an interpretation of the fall of man (in individualistic structures) and of redemption (through socialist structures)—an interpretation which is clearly at loggerheads with the faith.

From a philosophical point of view, socialism defines itself as a theology of society *for* man, which refuses to be a society *through* man. Between the *necessity* of social justice and the contingencies of personal freedoms, socialism seeks to impose the first *against* the second, despairing of turning contingent freedoms toward the communal practice of justice.

From a juridical point of view, socialism appears as the

---

[13] *Quadragesimo Anno*, no. 119.

progressive absorption of the domain of private rights into the domain of public rights (in contra-distinction to individualism, which absorbs vast forms of public rights into private rights).

From a sociological point of view, socialism corresponds to a society where the sense of duty is in a state of serious decay. Men in this state prefer to trust the justice of structures rather than the virtue of their fellow man, even when this virtue is strongly upheld by law.

From an economic point of view, socialism corresponds to the negation of the person as the subject of the social economy. The subject is the obligatory group, small or large, i.e., the group possessing public rights.

I refrain from developing certain of the points mentioned, but these could help those who might be tempted to marry Christianity and socialism to discover what a hopeless religious situation would be brought about thereby.

Thus Pius XI states:

> Now when false principles are thus mitigated and in some sense waived, the question arises, or rather is unwarrantably proposed in certain quarters, whether the principles of Christian truth also could not be somewhat moderated and attenuated, so as to meet socialism as it were halfway upon common ground. Some are enticed by the empty hope of gaining in this way the socialists to our cause. But such hope is vain. Those who wish to be apostles amongst the socialists must preach the Christian truth whole and entire, openly and sincerely, without any connivance at error. If they wish in truth to be heralds of the Gospel, let their first endeavor be to convince socialists that their demands, in so far as they are just, are defended much more cogently by the principles of Christian faith, and are promoted much more efficaciously by the power of Christian charity.[14]

Openness to the world does not change anything. It only challenges us to be more concerned about communicating Christian hope to those—numerous as they may be—who are led, through the incessant barrage of propaganda, to place their hope in socialism.

---

[14] *Quadragesimo Anno*, no. 116.

6

Socialism with a Christian Face

New Presentation of Religion
The Key Points of the New Theology
What I Believe

Is the "socialism with a human face" that has been proposed compatible with the simple sense of faith?

It is when one looks at a town from a certain altitude that one can best grasp its total configuration. Similarly, the main lines, the profile of a thought, a faith, a religion, are best apprehended if we regard them from a certain distance.

In confronting the authentic teaching of Jesus Christ and of His Church with the ideas being spread today concerning man's liberation, we can witness the development, not only of a clear exploitation of faith in the service of the socialist ideology, but also the birth of a new religious thought, a new faith which is no longer the one that has been transmitted to us—in short, which is no longer the Christian faith. Every detail of this development is subject to discussion, for the contingency and the complexity of things is often such that there is no room for discussion. As we are increasingly compelled to adopt a position on it, I shall attempt to sketch the silhouette of this thought, this faith, this new religion which is arising among us. Then

103

I shall evoke the one we believe in, today as yesterday, the true thought, the true faith, the true religion.

Presentation of a New Religion

The new religion urged upon us has been, I believe, objectively presented in *Les Etudes* of December 1970 by Louis de Vaucelles, under the title, "Notes after the Pastoral Session of Lourdes." I select this most typical passage by way of illustration:

> Credit should be given to the A.C.O. for having posed the problem with the greatest clarity in bringing out the inevitable conflict which it believes to exist between the neo-liberal humanism and the civilization which aims at promoting the workers' movement . . . .
>
> What is at stake is the destruction of a society dominated by money and lies. The means of action in this combat is the class struggle, which is presented by the A.C.O. not only as a fact which imposes itself on workers because of the oppression and exploitation under which they labor, but also as the very condition of their liberation. A worker-priest wrote in his report presented in Lourdes, "Class struggle can become a love impulse—even violent—to destroy the sin of this world, and to transform humanity into a fraternal and upright people."
>
> The interpellation of the A.C.O. is addressed primarily to Christians who do not endorse these views. In urging them to acknowledge that the constraints of capitalism weigh most heavily on the workers and threaten most their dignity, the movement refrains from condemning the "bourgeois" who, they believe, are themselves unconscious victims of the system and who also stand in need of material and spiritual liberation from the alienations into which they have sunk.
>
> Even from a purely secular point of view, is it not, in the last analysis, in the interests of the leading classes that they should reflect seriously on their place and role in society? On the other hand, all strata of society, including the working class, should be encouraged to further the advances to which the Gospel invites us.

A superficial reading of this text may lead us to believe that what is being discussed is a simple summary of Marxist-Leninist

104

thought, in its most orthodox garb. We find here the fundamental analysis of society as consisting of inevitably opposed classes, the ultimate character of the present aspect of this class struggle.[1] Moreover, we find here, too, the claim that capitalism is the profound cause of any and every social disorder because of "its constraints which weigh most heavily on the workers and threaten most their dignity." Here again we find, under a new name, the key thesis of historical materialism: alienation, on both the material and spiritual plane. In it, too, is to be found the central historical intuition of Marxism-Leninism: the history of the world divided by an irreducible conflict between two epochs, the one preceding and the other following the advent of socialism. We find in it the claim that it is a social revolution, a temporal revolution, a combat, a class struggle, which will realize effectively and fundamentally "the destruction of a society dominated by money and lies." Finally, we find in it a call to the bourgeois, and here more particularly "to those Christians who do not share these views," not that they may expound their reasons, but in order "to urge them to recognize that the constraints of capitalism . . .," etc.[2] Marx explains that "as soon as the class struggle reaches its decisive hour, the process of decay of the dominating class will assume such violence, that a small fraction of this class will sever itself from it and rally the revolutionary class, the class that carries the promise of the future."

Once again, there is nothing original in all this. It is a conscientious, clear and concise summary of Marxism-Leninism, which is to be found in all textbooks. What is in question, however, is not simply that ideology as such, and this is why I am so insistent on this point. What truly matters is that we are dealing with a new Christian thought, a new Christian faith, a new Christian religion.

I call it this not primarily or essentially because it is the Workers' Catholic Action which presents this thought to the bishops; not even because (as the studies tell us very seriously) "the summons of the A.C.O. is primarily addressed to Christians who

---

[1] Cf. *The Manifesto of the Communist Party*, Social Editions, p. 15.

[2] *Ibid.*, p. 24.

do not share our views, while urging them to acknowledge that they should change their faith!" I insist upon this point because we are dealing with a theology which is spreading full speed within the Church, and still more by a practical grafting than by public and theoretical statements.

It is this theology which we shall now explain. It has manifested itself at Lourdes, as reported in the *Studies (Etudes)*. But it is ubiquitous, and infiltrates movements, sermons, even families, in the name of the Gospel.

The Key Features of the New Theology

At the starting point of this new theology we find an affirmation introduced as a fact, and which dominates everything which follows: an historical struggle is taking place whose aim is the liberation of the working class from whatever oppresses it. The working world has attained practically nothing except through struggle, strike, etc. The workers' organizations grant the working world a hope of salvation, a liberation from every type of oppression. These organizations seek the establishment of a society of free and responsible men. The majority of the workers estimate that this project cannot be realized within the existing economic system. In spite of certain organizations ruled by a minority, who believe that the capitalistic system is susceptible to reform, it is the system itself which is challenged by the majority. It seeks power, whether in the quality of its working class, or in the framework of a classless society.

Such is the incontestable fact, the imperative point of departure of the new faith. On this basis, we must inquire into how Christians—mostly lay and poor, some militants, a few priests— live the death and resurrection of Jesus Christ in the class struggle.

According to this interpretation, the sin of the world does not lie in the loss of original justice through our first parents. It is the monetary oppression exercized by one class over another. This version claims its support in the Psalms, the prayer of Job, chapter 24, where Job revolts and refuses to accept the fate of the poor and appeals to God. This is the foundation of a "theology of sin" identified with a capitalist regime, and a theology of liberation

106

which applies, selectively, only to those oppressed by the capitalistic system.

"The great sin," "the sin of the world," and to put it quite plainly, the only sin, is social injustice. No mention is made of ungodliness. God Himself only knows the sins of injustice produced by a capitalistic system, and which negate His creation.

The theology of Redemption derives from it: it tends to identify redemption through Christ with a sort of new social regime in which labor difficulties, housing crises, illiteracy, and so forth will be done away with.

The cross of Jesus Christ will no longer be seen as the instrument of redemption. Rather redemption will come through a violent class struggle, the struggle of a people for its liberation. According to the new religion, a successful Lent will basically consist of the preaching of temporal liberation, rather than the commemoration of the flight from Egypt, the passage from slavery to the Promised Land, which is at the origin of the feast of Easter. The celebration of Easter will itself be the passage from the old life of sinner and oppressor to the new life of temporal liberation of a society that has become Christian to the very extent that it has become socialist.

In this way, collective action and the struggle between the classes will appear to generate moral life, spiritual life, theological life.

What I Believe

I have received a faith from the Church of Jesus Christ and through my parents and teachers which has little in common with the one I have just elaborated. It is not my task to refute the religion proposed by the chaplains of the A.C.O., of members of the national organizations of working priests, of militants who ponder over "the birth of the Church in the heart of the class struggle" (sic), of the session of Mouvaux, of Lourdes, or of anywhere else. I leave this work to those who are called to it.

On the other hand, as a baptized, confirmed layman, I feel that I am called upon to give testimony to what I believe. Present circumstances make this an imperative duty.

I

I believe that the most momentous event in the history of the world is the birth, death and resurrection of the incarnate Word, Jesus Christ, and that it is this event and this event alone which lies at the heart of the Catholic faith. Any kind of identification of the death and resurrection of Jesus Christ with a politico-social prophecy of the death of a capitalist sinner and oppressor and of a resurrection to one or another form of socialism, democratic or not, strikes me as opposed to the Catholic faith, which it reduces to merely temporal dimensions and subjects to ideological ends.

I believe that to work toward the establishment of a society in which *personal* initiative and responsibility are gradually and radically eliminated is a project which runs contrary to faith, for it tends to *create a society in which justice will be guaranteed, without there being any need for the interior life of the soul, and amendment of the will.* Distributive and general justice will be guaranteed everywhere, through the perfection of collective constraints which will replace the freedoms of persons or private groups. A gigantic, anonymous social structure will assume responsibility for the just distribution of work and consumer goods. This will be accomplished without the need for each man to practice justice freely and in cooperation with grace.

Such a "redemption" is to my mind sheer pharisaism. Here man, as person, refuses to acknowledge himself to be a sinner. He also refuses to accept the consequences of sin.

This is no way implies that we must accept the existence of human misery, the lower classes, the slums. But it is one thing to fight for a right, and another to deprive man of his rights.

II

I believe what the Church teaches with respect to original sin, i.e., that through this sin man has lost supernatural life, and that as a result, it is no longer possible for him to enter by himself into immediate communion with the personal life of the Holy Trinity. Moreover, original sin has weakened human nature, but it has not corrupted it. It has weakened both our intelligence and our will, but, within certain limits, man is still capable of receiving the lost supernatural goods when they are given back through God's grace. In no case can this teaching be further enlightened by or in any way reconciled with the Marxist theory of alienation and the concomitant hope of a socialist liberation.

III

I believe that no salvation is to be expected except salvation in Jesus Christ, and that it is impossible ever to find an order of communal life superior to the one inaugurated by the Savior Himself, in associating the baptized to His death and resurrection, making of each of us a new man[3] without racial, national or class distinctions. I believe that the baptized faithful form together a new people, for it is Jesus Christ who " . . . is the peace between us, and has made the two into one and broken down the barrier which used to keep them apart, actually destroying in his own person the hostility caused by the rules and decrees of the law. This was to create one single new man in Himself out of the two of them and by restoring peace through the cross, to unite them both in a single body and reconcile them with God. In his own person he killed the hostility."[4]

IV

I believe that it is the New Testament and its message of love and mercy which sheds light on and accomplishes what is prophesied and promised in the Old; I reject the interpretation which claims that the message of justice contained in the Old Testament enlightens and accomplishes what is said in the New. I believe, moreover, that the beatitudes referring to poverty and justice cannot be systematically severed from the other beatitudes with which they constitute the Good News.

V

I believe that the most grievous sin is the one which brings men to refuse to adore, from the depth of their souls, the Just God, the God of Love, Creator and Savior of the world. Other sins, those related to money, the flesh or pride of the spirit, exist first in the heart of men, not in social structures. I believe that Jesus' preference for the poor implies an invitation to immolation and

[3] Colossians 3:9-10.
[4] Ephesians 2:14-16.

self-sacrifice and, as a result, a call to reasonable temporal action to fight against misery and suffering which exist to a greater or less degree in all classes, and in all walks of life. This preference for the poor can never, under any circumstances, be legitimately presented as a justification of violence toward a certain class designated as the oppressors, or as the justification of militant Christians to harden themselves, within the Church, to the imitation of Jesus Christ.

VI

I believe that society is one moral body: the social body, and that far from breaking it down into inherently opposed classes, we should try to reconstitute it in reciprocal justice, according to the explicit teaching ot Pope Pius XI, in order to bear out in the social body what the apostle said of the Mystical Body of Jesus Christ: "If we live by the truth and in love, we shall grow in all ways into Christ, who is the head by whom the whole body is fitted and joined together, every joint adding its own strength, for each separate part to work according to its function. So the body grows until it has built itself up, in love."[5]

VII

If liberal individualism in the West and socialist totalitarianism in the East torture, dislocate or corrupt the social body today, I believe that it is not due to social or economic systems, but primarily to men's ungodliness, their avarice, their impurity, their rebelliousness. They call their greed "consumer society." They call their impurity "erotic liberation." They call their rebelliousness "controversy" or "reexamination of questions."

To go back to the Gospel does not mean to baptize sins and vices, as is done in the individualistic, liberal society of the West. Neither does it mean transforming society into a sort of ant hill, nor interpreting the evangelical message through Marxist slogans about class struggle, alienation, and redemptive socialism. To go back to the Gospel of Jesus Christ means, in cooperation with grace, to work alone, with God, then together with the baptized,

---

[5] Ephesians 4:15-16.

then to give testimony before those who do not yet believe—to live the counsel of St. Paul to the Colossians:

> That is why you must kill everything in you that belongs only to earthly life: fornication, impurity, guilty passion, evil desires and especially greed, which is the same thing as worshipping a false god; all this is the sort of behavior that makes God angry. And it is the way in which you used to live when you were surrounded by people doing the same thing, but now you, of all people, must give all these things up: getting angry, being bad-tempered, spitefulness, abusive language and dirty talk; and never tell each other lies. You have stripped off your old behavior with your old self, and you have put on a new self which will progress toward true knowledge the more it is renewed in the image of its creator; and in that image there is no room for distinction between Greek and Jew, between the circumcised and the uncircumcized, or between barbarian and Scythian, slave and free man. There is only Christ: he is everything and he is in everything.[6]

The necessary and legitimate promotion of the causes of industrial workers cannot be severed from the promotion of the causes of agriculturalists, artisans and those in professions of service. Moreover, these professional problems are no more urgent than another class of problems which pertain to all social strata: old age, ill-adapted youth, broken homes, academic freedom in schools and universities. All these problems face us today, and in all systems. But these are more likely to be solved if the Christian faith is authentic, respected, and freely practiced. It is the divine life in souls, the meditation upon and concrete application of the social doctrine of the Church, which will allow the realization, day by day, of true social progress, in cooperation with natural law.

I know for a fact that my reaction to the "new Christianity," cast in a Marxist-Leninist mold, is not isolated! The silent majority of the Christians of France, in the name of the Word of God, *choose* the social doctrine of the Church, for there is one. It, and it alone, is the perfect way to communion with the God who has come to live among us.

---

[6] Colossians 3:5-11.

111

7

Anatomy of Totalitarianism

The Three Powers
The Necessary Separation of These Powers

Can the present threat of totalitarianism help us discover guidelines worthy of God and man?

In the nineteenth century, too many churchmen endorsed economic liberalism. This ideology, politically imposed by the French Revolution, presented itself as an accepted idea with a claim to historical evidence. Due to moral weakness and preoccupation with a distorted conception of the apostolate, numerous priests and, alas, bishops, refrained from raising their voices against an individualistic economic system which made private ownership the only axis of the social order. The rise and development of an industrial proletariat resulted from this, and was considered by the liberals to be an inevitable consequence of the sacrosanct natural law.

History repeats itself. It will teach us that in the twentieth century too many churchmen have endorsed socialism and communism, or at least multiplied intellectual distinctions to push their flock in that direction. This collectivist ideology, politically imposed by the Russian and Chinese revolutions, imposes itself today due to the accepted idea of the fatality of contemporary change. Due to their weakness of character and their ignorance (which in social matters is often great), numerous priests and, alas, bishops,

113

fail to raise their voices against an economic system which makes public collectivism the only axis of the social order. From this results the irrational ascendancy of an omnipotent and irreversible political totalitarianism, which Christians associated with or even committed to the ideologies of socialism and communism end by helping.

The Three Powers

Contrary to the claims of Marxism, society cannot be basically defined in terms of class relationships. This situation could be found only within a framework of pure or nearly pure liberalism. We are far from that. Our contemporary society basically defines itself, rather, through the relationship of powers. This is a fact, whether we like it or not. And while extensive schematizing is often unfortunate, we are compelled by necessity to recognize today the existence of three great powers, and various counter-powers which oppose them.

I. The Political Power

This is the oldest power, and the very notion of civilization demonstrates its profound purpose. This is the power which undertakes the management of the public good while respecting the private liberties of the citizens. In the past its primary areas of influence within the state were the administration of justice, finance, and military protection. Since Montesquieu, the legislative, executive and judiciary powers have been distinguished within it, and under these basic distinctions, various subdivisions.

II. The Economic Power

The economic power came into being with industrial capitalism, a little over a hundred years ago. The notion of enterprise is its most important aspect. Within the framework of individual liberties, and the liberty to make contracts, this power guarantees the adaptation of production to needs and distribution of buying power among families. Formerly divided among innumerable enterprises, this power has tended in the last fifty years to concen-

114

trate itself in the hands of financial oligarchies and monopolies.

III. The Cultural Power

This power, born with the "literary republic" or the intellectual magistery of the eighteenth century encyclopedists, has since constantly increased in importance, which by now has reached inordinate proportions. It is exercised by the controllers of television and radio broadcasts, the producers of films and records, the printers of newspapers, books and magazines, and the directors of publicity and fashion. Formerly the Church exercised an influence on both arts and letters. Today the opposite is true: it is the cultural power which exercises its influence on the Church, and has contributed to the growth of the crisis of faith. What we are dealing with now, however, is not a new spiritual power, but a purely aesthetic power, for its influence is exercised primarily in the name of the freedom and demands of art.

These three powers exist in a state of precarious equilibrium. Each of them is curbed, disputed, and at times defeated by one or more of the others.

Guarded groups such as the Free Masons, the clandestine apparatus of the Communist Party in its various centers of activity, as well as the outspoken organized opposition, exercise pressures on the political power. The powerful economic counter-power of the trade unions brings pressure to bear on the economic power. Petitions, letters, and various other means are employed by the silent majority (whose name expresses their strength of number and the weakness of their available modes of expression) to exercise pressure on the aesthetic power, with strikingly unequal results.

Brief as this sketch may be, it represents a faithful picture of the deep-rooted reality which rigorous scientific analysis of our society reveals. In liberal democracies with a high standard of living, the Marxist conceptualization of classes no longer corresponds to anything. This conceptualization cannot even adequately help determine whether the heads of industry should be regarded as a new kind of exploited people, or as capitalist decision-makers. In fact, they form an integral part of the economic power.

115

The Necessity for Separation of Powers

The key to the problem of social justice in a society of this kind lies in the *de jure* and *de facto* relationships among these three powers. These relationships should tend to bring into play the dynamism of private liberties in order to establish an equitable prosperity, respecting the common good.

If the emphasis is placed exclusively on the freedom of owners, the individualistic aspect of democracy is reinforced. The economic power then tends to guarantee the neutrality and even the sympathy of the political power and, in extreme cases, aims at exercising partial control over it. In the purely liberal state of nineteenth century Western Europe the right of association was abolished, and the state was reduced to the role of policeman, responsible for putting thieves into jail. The peasants and workers were largely proletarized. Private ownership alone—the foundation of the economic power—enjoyed absolute and sacred rights.

What those Christians, lay or religious, who today support socialism to a greater or less degree, fail to see is that in the long run they are working toward plunging the whole of society into a totalitarianism which is much more dehumanizing than the one produced by the mechanism of pure liberalism. A century of struggle has been necessary in order to come out of the latter, in returning to the state the role of social legislator, to the workers the right of association, to the Church her doctrinal influence. For, if the nineteenth century committed the mistake of making private ownership the *only* pivot of social structure, enslaving the state and proletarizing families, the experience of the twentieth century shows that the abolition of private property is a symmetrical error.

Let us be very specific. In abolishing private property, one abolishes the actual power of persons or of private groups over means of production, and indirectly their authority over the persons who work by means of these enterprises. But the necessity is not thereby eliminated for a technical hierarchy, or the responsibility of commanding; in short, for the inevitable subordination of workers to the decision-makers. However, if the suppliers of work are no longer subordinate to the holders of capital (or to any form of private authority which issues from it independently of public authority), they will necessarily fall under a form of public authority—which is to say, directly or indirectly under the power of a political implementation of a collectivistic ideology.

The subjection under which churches, intellectuals and artists labor in socialistic countries is well known. They have the benefit of no statutes except those granted through favor or negotiations. This is an inevitable consequence of the collectivity of goods, and the correlative suppression of the right to private ownership. The incorporation of the economic and cultural powers into the political one constitutes, therefore, in its very structure, the essence of totalitarianism.

An independent political power which respects the freedom of the other two powers while regulating and correcting them is one thing. A totalitarian, unrivalled power to which everything else is subjected is quite another. Therefore, the scientific analysis both suggested and confirmed by the study of facts in their correlation, reveals two inescapable facts: when the balance between the state (political power) and private ownership (economic power) is weighted in favor of the latter, money enslaves the state and exploits the workers. This is the social history of the nineteenth century. When the balance between the state and private ownership is weighted in favor of the former, the separation of the three powers ceases to exist and the cultural and economic powers are incorporated and monopolized by the political power.

Hopefully the Christians who militate for the socialist way will learn that the most inhuman of social injustices consists in yielding to one central power the powers of the state, heads of enterprises, spiritual leaders and cultural leaders. Hopefully they will realize that this absolute concentration of powers is the *automatic* result of the abolition of private ownership of the means of production. Hopefully they will become conscious of the fact that the social order inspired by the Gospel *implies* the liberty of the children of God, in the social order as well as in the spiritual order.

Perhaps I shall be answered once again, "In the name of the Gospel, you admit the actual liberal capitalism and identify yourself with flagrant social injustices, etc." I have already said that this is not the case.

As I have mentioned above, contemporary French society is far removed from pure liberalism. It is steeped in interventionism—already partly socialized—and its most serious problems are not those most frequently mentioned by the demagogues. Nonetheless, we are called upon to work consistently to lay bare unjust social situations, the new poor, hidden sufferings. We need reform!

It is to be desired that the opposition, whatever it may be, proclaims what is overlooked, omitted or refused by the government. We favor the pursuit of efficacious action leading to concrete and precise reforms.

For example: The actual separation of the three powers, far from being abolished, should be reinforced along hierarchical lines. This is the key to any reform capable of fostering the development of justice and liberty. The political power must become more and more independent of the other two. And it must possess this independence in order to establish conditions which will allow the other two to develop freely. It would thus lie within the realm of the political power to limit their excesses and to curb them with severity, if need be. The intrusions of the wielders of economic power upon the holders of political power need to be denounced and stopped. But it is nothing short of preposterous to believe that these excesses can be remedied by absorbing the economic power into the political one. The will to power is overextended as soon as one of these two powers absorbs the other.

Moreover, a social order respectful of the dignity of all persons must necessarily imperatively require that private property be neither absorbed by the state, nor the state by private property. Both of them, as well as the family itself (toward which they are ordered), are institutions which cannot be considered in isolation, but only in their organic relationship.

In feudal France, a few powerful families who monopolized rural property as well as local political authority, endeavored to outweigh the authority of the monarchist state.

In liberal France, the increasing fortunes of the owners of financial, industrial and commercial capital undermined the authority of the republican state.

In a France manaced by socialism, what looms on the horizon is the absorption by the state of private property and the liberty of thought within families. This is the technique of totalitarianism, which is another word for slavery.

It suffices to meditate on this evolution to understand that the sociological law which flows out of it shows that the dignity of the human person can be preserved only when the family, property and the state, far from being absorbed by one another, remain each in its own sphere, as complementary elements of the social order.

To give a concrete illustration, the worker today is, as citizen, subject to state laws. He is also subject, by contract, to a private authority as wage earner in a private sector. The very day that public authority—directly or indirectly—relegates the economic power in enterprises to the state, *the freedom enjoyed by all men, resulting from the separation of powers, will be irretrievably annihilated.* Already in France management in the public sector is merely a cover-up for the state.

A wage earner who has a dispute with his employer can work for someone else, but when the employer cannot be distinguished from the popular collectivity, under whatever name, this freedom is forfeited.

Similarly, the right to strike is feasible only if the two powers coexist. Wherever the political authority absorbs the whole economic power, the concrete struggle of the working class to effect change becomes impossible, since *by definition* it is the proletariat that controls this power. The only recourse of the working man against "the dictatorship of the proletariat" is to let himself be killed, as is the case in East Germany, in Budapest, in Prague, in Poland. . . .

Similarly, the inventiveness, the creativeness of free enterprise will no longer be able to exercise itself with a living economic reality. It will be forced to go through the intermediary of the one, unique, politico-economic power. If a genius inventor happens to be a revisionist, too bad for his genius! If the offices responsible for receiving his request are congested, lazy or sectarian, too bad for the invention! By contrast, in a system of separation between political and economic powers, innumerable avenues of recourse are open to him and the possible alternatives are truly democratic.

Those who talk about a human socialism find themselves, as we saw, confronted with a choice. Either they must abolish the right of ownership of means of production, in which case the socialism which fuses the economic and political powers into one boss-state can never lay claim to being human, or they must uphold private property, as in German socialism. But in the latter case, the system would no longer be truly socialistic.

Incidentally, it is impossible to abolish private ownership of the means of production without incorporating the cultural power into the politico-economic power. We must remember that this power is both the most apparent and the least recognized for what it is. Posters, jingles, fashions, magazines, broadcasts, the aesthetic climate, are all factors which select, moderate, suppress, distort, or magnify in order to shape an entertainment or pleasure, and therefore manipulate—often without his being aware of it—the reader, listener, spectator, or consumer. The latter believe themselves to be free as they buy, view, hear or read only what they choose. But they do not begin to comprehend how much is concealed from them, the powerful implantation of ideas in what is shown to them, the neuro-physical action exercized on them by what is told or sung to them. With the weight of real psychologically persuasive power, the media insinuate a certain morality, spread a way of life, and do not hesitate to multiply directors of consciences, both masculine and feminine.

It is therefore inevitable, as soon as the system of private property is abolished, that press, radio, television, movies, publications, records, publicity, and all the forms of intellectual and artistic expressions, can no longer exist except through the collectivity. Every book, every broadcast will require a political decision, taken within a collectivist universe, both homogeneous and hermetically sealed. From then on, cultural and intellectual contributions, decisions about nominations, and credits granted will depend upon an uncontrollable administration, if not on purges. No free cultural or intellectual initiative will be possible, starting with a "free" school.

It goes without saying that in a collectivist universe, there is no room for any authentic religious freedom, because religious grounds will belong not to private groups but to the public collectivity. In the best of cases, this collectivity will authorize the lending of churches to the faithful, monasteries to the monks, and so forth. *But they can do so only under the condition that the churches forsake teaching that private ownership is a natural right of man.* Religion then is subjected to the worst possible violence: the buying of its own freedom at the price of its complicity with the technique of slavery applied to a whole people.

The Social Body and the Mystical Body

"That they may be one, Father, as we are one."

Any social order that truly respects man's dignity must be based on the teaching the Church has given us from its beginning, a teaching that Pius XII summarized in declaring, "Marriage and the family, the state, private ownership, tend, by their very nature, to form and develop man as a person, to protect him, and render him capable of contributing, through his free collaboration and his personal responsibility, to the upholding and development (both of which are also personal) of social life."[1]

Private ownership must be extended as widely as possible, and ever further, so that all families, including the new ones being founded continually, may quickly establish a basis of legitimate independence and healthy freedom, and at the same time the opportunity to assume the responsibility of management of their own possessions. John XXIII asked that the capital of societies be distributed among the multitude of families in all classes of society. It is at this point that a call for fairer distribution of goods must be launched, and that the state, in collaboration with both families and enterprises, must aim at the improvement of justice in the collaboration of liberties within the necessary framework of separation of powers.

Pius XI, followed by Pius XII, described at length the timely formulation of this collaboration, capable of granting social life its

---

[1] Pius XII, broadcast on December 24, 1953.

121

living texture. They showed that whereas a single enterprise belongs legitimately to its private owners—individuals, families, or numerous stockholders—the profession, on the other hand, or the entire economy, belong to all those who collaborate with it, whatever their position on the socio-economic scale.

In conclusion, I must insist upon one fact that has impressed me particularly. In choosing to shed light on two aspirations or our contemporary society in *Octogesima Adveniens,* Paul VI has selected the longing for equality and the desire for participation. These two aspirations coincide precisely with the crucial discourse delivered by Pius XII on May 7, 1949—and here again, we must admire the way in which Paul VI, under a new form, remains within the strict tradition of the Church. In realizing the fundamental equality of workers and heads of enterprise, Pius XII emphasized, "They are collaborators in a common work. They eat—so to speak—at the same table, for they live, in the last analysis, from the clear and global profit of the national income. Each of them receives his income, and from this point of view, their mutual relationship in no way puts one at the service of the other." He proceeded to develop the theme of participation: "But as the interest is common, why not translate it in a common expression? Why would it not be legitimate to attribute to wage earners a fair share of responsibility in the formation and development of the national economy?"

These words sound like a premonition of this explosion of longing for equality and participation which has been manifested in 1968, in their most profound significance. We see today that this double aspiration leads to the appropriation of the whole economy by all those involved in it on a parity level; this applies to both the professional and inter-professional levels.

To the extent that Paul VI's letter renews the affirmation that "one and the same Christian faith can lead to a variety of engagements,"[2] one can understand that if the fraternal love implied in the Gospel radically precludes class struggles, it can, on the other hand, lead committed Christians on either the Right or

---

[2] *Ibid.,* no. 50.

the Left[3] to work toward bending the parties for which they work toward a synthesis of their aspirations: free enterprise in an organized profession.

It is normal and just that, within the domain of private ownership, an enterprise, whether the property of a few or of many owners, be administered by them or by their trustees according to the rules of a healthy market economy.

It is normal and just that in the domain of public right, a collaboration of classes, of workers of all ranks, be initiated step by step through contracts freely negotiated. This will lead, as has been empirically shown, to a progressive co-management of professions and of the whole of economy.

It is normal and just that the state favor, instigate, dedicate such contracts and such agreements between patrons and unions, and that, in an authentic freedom, it acts as arbiter when called upon to do so. In such a collaboration of the classes, even when difficult, tense, or cumbersome, *concrete* problems will be solved, one by one; and the equity of a fairer distribution of tasks and goods will be progressively realized, with each of the participants on both professional and inter-professional levels bringing out a point of view foreign to the others.

Should this be called today "the social program of the Church?" I truly do not think so. The Church has a missionary role to fulfill toward men. In them, enlightened by the Holy Spirit, she wants to trace the main lines of the society to come. But no doubt it remains essential, in the spirit of the preaching of the Gospel, to work toward the realization in the social body of what the apostle says of the Mystical Body of Christ: "If we live by the truth and in love, we shall grow in all ways into Christ, who is the head by whom the whole body is fitted and joined together, every joint adding its own strength, for each separate part to work according to its function. So the body grows until it has built itself up, in love."[4] Is this not a necessary and natural condition of the application of theological life to society? And can the Christian live other than by faith, hope and charity?

---

[3] This will be examined in *Left and Right,* to be published.
[4] Ephesians 4:15-16.